DASHI

DASHI

M.E.J. Powell

Kingfisher Sparrow 2017
Copyright © 2017 by M.E.J. Powell
ALL RIGHTS RESERVED

For more information to reproduce selections from this book write to Permissions@KingfisherSparrow.ca

KingfisherSparrow.ca

Cataloging-in Publication Data
Powell, M.E.J., 1966 –
Dashi.
1. Powell, M.E.J. (Mark Evan James), Characters–Dashi.
2. Powell, M.E.J. (Mark Evan James), Philosophy and ethics.
3. Philosophy in literature.
4. Philosophy.   I. Title.

ISBN 978-1-7750848-1-5

(unleaded & no pubic shaming)

DASHI

I
Dashi and the Master

Dashi went to the mountain with dried fish in his pack.

He found the master seated under a tree by a river.

"Master, I am troubled. The world is full of suffering."
"Why interfere? What business is it of yours?"

"But master, the people are in need, is there no value in helping."
"They will eat you skin and bones. Avoid them."

"Ahh... you mean one should deny one's desires?"
"Bees find the right flower for nectar. Birds find the right tree for their nests."

"But, I'm virtually an outcast, I belong nowhere."
"Then make your home anywhere you want."

"Are you telling me that I should

ignore how badly other people treat me?"

"Ah... Here is the real heart of the matter. It isn't respect or commiseration or understanding you want - it's agreement. Being a pigeon among cats is obviously dangerous. Being a cat among pigeons is less obviously dangerous. Value those who value what you value."

"Master your teachings seem terribly selfish to me, I do not understand why you are held in such repute."

The master stood and Dashi noted he was the same height as he.

"Hold my walking stick," said the master, and took off his robes. Standing naked before Dashi, he said, "For me this stick is long enough and for you it is too short."

"Life is sweet," said the master and slipped into the water for a swim.

II
The Donkey and the Ditch

i

The master walked into town to get a small bag of rice, as much as he could carry all the way back to his mountain retreat. As he passed through the central square he saw young Dashi standing at the gates of the magistrate's mansion waving a red flag.

"What are you doing?" asked the old master.

"O... it's you," Dashi replied, "I am challenging injustice."

"You are baiting a bull. When it comes charging out, do you believe you'll be able to hop on its back?"

Dashi shuffled his feet nervously. "I do not know what will happen to me, but I don't care. I have to stand for my values."

"You do care, you just don't think you do, and that is something different. Besides this isn't standing for your values it is standing for your outrage."

Dashi squinted. "Yes, I am outraged because my values have been challenged. I am flying my flag."

"Exactly, as I said, outrage, not values. And it is outrage the magistrate will feel when you are seen standing out here flouting authority – only the flag that will be flying is your skin!"

"What should I do then?" asked Dashi, "I have to do something."

"Just what I have been saying, know your values. Only then can you know the values of the magistrate."

"I know my values," said Dashi, "Just yesterday they dragged away my brother for poaching deer from the forest! That is what I am protesting."

The master shook his head, but then cocked his ear, "I fear I am not getting through to you." With his staff he swiftly knocked young Dashi's legs out from under him making him fall to the ground with a crash. "How clumsy, here let me help you up," said the master and he offered his hand. Dashi reached up and the master jerked Dashi forward, quickly head butting the young protestor who fell back in a dazed heap. Dashi's face began to turn red with anger.

The sound of hoof falls was now evident, as a troop of cavalry poured into the square and surrounded them, "What's going on here?" asked the head guard. Dashi looked on in horror.

Out of the master's mouth came the common vernacular. "My stupid lunk head servant has gotten drunk again. Look his face is red. And he keeps falling down."

"It is unlawful to be drunk in a public place. Arrest him!" And no sooner had the captain of the guard said this then three of the cavalry dismounted and put young Dashi in irons.

"Wait... how will I carry my rice back to my mountain retreat? It is very heavy for an old man like myself to carry all that way," said the master to the captain of the guard.

The head guard said brusquely, "You will have to find another who can do that for you."

"But," said the master, "It is hard to find someone to do such work. If he was any good at being anything better than a pack horse he'd be apprenticing. It's easy to find a fool, but to find a fool who knows he's a fool is much harder. Please allow my pack horse to carry the rice for me."

The head guard laughed. "He still broke the law. He was drunk."

"Captain, does that law apply to pack horses?" asked the master.

The head guard and his men laughed. "No, it does not apply to dumb animals," he chuckled, "All right. Release him."

All the time Dashi had been quaking uncontrollably, and did not stop despite having the manacles removed.

"Thank you for your kindness," said the master, "I feel this is exactly the kind of sobering experience that will train this burdensome beast."

The head guard nodded at the master and then glared, pointing right at Dashi in warning. The troop rode on, chuckling. One of the guard threw Dashi a carrot.

The master picked it up. "That will go well in the stew."

"Thank you for saving me, master. I did not understand. I am in your debt."

"That's what touching the ground can do for you," said the master. "At least now you know the difference between outrage and what you truly value. I for one value humour, even at your expense – as I guessed the captain would."

"I see," said Dashi.

"Do you see?" challenged the master, "Here is the mansion of a magistrate. What is valued here?"

"Power," said Dashi, bitterly.

"That is one likely value," said the master, "Come now young Dashi, you can dine with me this evening. The flag will make a good sling for your strong back. I am going to buy the largest bag of rice I can find."

ii

Dashi was massaging his sore back, looking out over the fire at the night sky above the mountain.

"You are broody," said the master smiling, "Are you going to lay the egg or just sit there?"

Dashi half smirked, "How can you be so calm when the world is so corrupt? They tax the food right out of our bellies. They treat us worse than dogs."

"Ah..." said the master, "Indeed corrupt. What would you do?"

"For one, I'd punish all the wrong doers."

Master said, "I see. How would you assess that?"

"It is plain for people to see the wrong of someone who steals and harms," asserted Dashi.

The master nodded, "Go on."

"It is simple," Dashi said, waggling his finger at the master as he enumerated. "Crime is defined by the victim. First does it make the other feel bad? Second does it lessen their dignity? And third does it rob them of some freedom? Intentionally doing those things is a worse crime than unintentionally, but any of those are conditions enough for guilt."

"Thinking of the magistrate," noted the master. "What do you propose if these wrong doers are found guilty?"

"They would be punished. Some might just be fined, but for others public shaming or imprisonment."

"Not death?" asked the master sighing.

Dashi paused. He put his lecturing finger down. "Perhaps," came his evasive reply.

The master looked upward, gazing at the stars. Seemingly searching for something there. "I once knew a woman who wanted a better husband. It wasn't that he was a bad husband, and he had a very nice little home on top of a mountain. But she was dissatisfied. It made her feel bad - to think she could have better. It was a loss to her dignity - to be seen with someone of lowered station than the one to which she aspired. And it robbed her of the freedoms - that she thought she would have. Should the husband be punished?"

"mmmm..." mumbled Dashi. And then after a moment. "I am sorry for your loss."

"Don't be," said the master, "that is my most cherished lesson."

Dashi turned his thoughts inward for a moment. "So what happened to her?"

"She found a better husband, one that had power, with the bigger house. He died. But she wasn't happy, so she tried with the next one, and found he wasn't so interested, so she got rid of him. Now she has the big house all to herself.

"As a powerful woman people are constantly coming with requests of this and that. Her old friends who liked her for who she was are long gone, replaced by those who like being near someone of her status. She has to constantly put on a show - or lose face.

"This requires a great deal of money. She squeezes all the people in the properties she oversees. Feeling bad, loss of dignity and freedom - she has given these first to herself and then to those below her. What do you judge should be her punishment?"

Dashi was quiet.

"Come, young Dashi. Don't be bashful now. What's your verdict?" urged the master.

Dashi sighed. "Well, she is oppressing those beneath her, so there should be some form of censure."

"A public shaming then. That would make her feel bad and lessen her dignity. What about the punishment for what she did to herself?" said the master.

Dashi began a reply then stopped. "Oh..." he said, "Master, I fear I did not know what I was saying."

The master leaned forward on his staff. "Explain yourself," he said softly but with authority.

"I said it was wrong to make others feel bad, to rob them of dignity and freedom, and that is just what I have proposed for their punishments."

"Let the punishment fit the crime?" suggested the master.

"No," said Dashi, "then whoever is punishing is merely reinforcing the idea that those with power can do these things."

"Doesn't might make right?" asked the master.

Dashi shook his head. "It doesn't. Now I see, master." He returned his gaze to the stars. "I think my heart is full of bad intentions. Can you help me?"

The master put his stick down firmly, startling Dashi, "No!" said the master, "'Bad intentions'... Ha. Don't you see? - All you have done is flip from magistrate to martyr. In your imaginings you sit as a great judge, wielding power like a scythe - but secretly you want to believe the true enemy is power itself, and not the hand that wields it – then you transform yourself conveniently into its victim.

"Secondly, you assume you know what 'wrong' is. Your rules catch up in their net: impoverished husbands, gouging landlords, and the self deluded."

"I need fairer rules," admitted Dashi.

"Rules applied fairly may still be terrible rules," said the master, "Judges aren't sent out fresh from their study of law because they require comprehension of people, not just rule following." He leaned forward. "Whatever wisdom can be said, there is a fool who can misinterpret it, and someone poisonous enough to do so on purpose. When multiple levels of meaning are reduced to one or two bloated ideas – they become the kind in which categorical wrongs lead to lots of rule making."

"Yes, my bad intensions," said Dashi, annoyed.

"You are not fit to judge others – or yourself," said the master. "You are asleep. You are dreaming of dead snakes biting their tails. Being hostile to yourself, for being hostile to others who are being hostile, is no antidote. It's not that you were in violation of valid rules. You make up the rules, and then scold yourself for your transgression. No wonder you want to disavow others.

"This is the present state of your consciousness. You are obsessed with what you think, but not the how. I tell you your mind is not free. Thus, if what I say bounces off your thick skull, there is nothing I can do. You must help yourself."

Dashi clasped his hands together. "What should I do to help myself, master?" he said humbly.

"First you need to free yourself from the hatred in your heart," said the master. "Meditate on the fire. Your discomfort is a hot coal inside you. Blow on it to make it burn hotter, to burn it away. Concentrate. Put your heart into it. Some part of the universe is not to your liking? – This is grieving it," he said. "After that, we can talk about understanding. I am going to bed now. When you come in, I suggest you sleep by the stove: it's warmest there."

And the master went inside.

iii

The birds were singing, and the sun dappled the ground as the two hiked among the pines, traversing the path to the high meadow where the master wished to gather plants for medicine. The master was silent.

Dashi on the other hand filled the air with speaking. "...still a community must have standards. So there must be law of some kind. They will have to come together and decide it. The majority will decide, what is favoured and what is not favoured. And instead of punishment, some way of reintegrating the offender into the community-"

"Stop," said the master. And Dashi halted in his tracks, the empty pack on his back flapping open. The master continued walking. "No, I mean, leave off your monologue. Look at the trees and listen to the sounds of the insects. Do you know where you are?"

Dashi looked left and right. "I am half-way up a mountain," he said catching up.

The master repeated himself with emphasis," Do you know where YOU are?"

"Ahh..." said Dashi, who then thought about his place in all of this.

They walked on higher and higher. The trail wound around old roots and Dashi found he had to watch his step. "Master, I am hiking up the mountain, with you, but part of me feels it is not my place, that I belong with other people. That is where I am."

"No," said the master simply. The meadow now in sight, he pulled himself up a rocky step with a nearby branch.

Dashi rebuked, returned to his thoughts. They entered the meadow and Dashi took off the pack. The master removed and rolled out a number of waxed skins he'd brought. He bent low, examining flowers. Some of which he picked, and gave to Dashi to place on the skins. When the pile was large enough, he instructed Dashi to wrap them and place them in the pack.

As they worked the master would sometimes instruct Dashi. "To a dog the world is full of smells. We know it's because of a highly specialised nose, but a dog just assumes this is the world.

"For you the world is full of categories, due to a highly specialized mind," the master handed Dashi a bundle of tiny flowers. "You talk about what there is to see, but it is the eye that perceives. If you do not know the eyes, then you do not understanding seeing. If you do not know the minds, you do not understand understanding." They continued in that way into the afternoon.

Later, the master took a skin and went off to look for a herb, leaving Dashi with the pack. The sun was warm, and the air fragrant. Dashi lay down in pink meadow flowers and beheld the blue sky where swallows sailed. He breathed deeply.

He did not notice that the master had returned and was standing behind him. "Softly, young Dashi, do you know where you are?"

"I am feeling peaceful. I am relaxed."

"Where were you before?"

Dashi thought back to the hike up. "I was thinking. I was analysing."

"Did you know this when you were in that state?" asked the master.

Dashi knew the answer, "No, I was just thinking," he said. "Should I think about my thinking while I am thinking?"

"Perish the thought," said the master, his voice low, "that would only serve to increase your prattle ten fold. I ask you to notice - that was one mind and this is another."

Dashi breathed in. Dashi breathed out. He felt his body lying on the ground. He felt the green tickle of the supple flower stems that touched his face and hands. "If that was thinking mind, what do I call this mind?" asked Dashi.

The master said, "It doesn't matter if you can name them, if you can't enter them, or leave them."

Dashi nodded, and squinted his eyes thinking deeply about that – so the master dumped leaves on his head.

iv

Dashi gathered sticks of wood. He did so slowly and sombrely. When he had enough, he carried them on his back. And when he'd returned from the forest to the master's home, he placed them into the woodpile, each according to its length, separated each according to its wood, taking a bundle of ten for inside.

Inside the master drank hot water, sitting by the window that looked down the valley to the town below. Dashi came in and sat down. He put his bundle down. The master gave Dashi his cup from which to drink. Dashi sighed, and the master raised his eyebrows and waited.

"Master, I do not love the magistrate."

"Did you expect to?" asked the master.

Dashi said, "Yes. I have been doing as you asked. I try to feel my body, be present, and when the anger comes, see how being angry fills me with a terrible feeling that I carry about. I see it is draining my strength. But I can't seem to let go of it."

The master took the cup back from Dashi, "Ah, did I show you any method for how to let this go?"

Dashi considered this. "No, Master," said

Dashi.

"What about the coal in the fire?" said the master.

"Oh, yes, that," said Dashi, "But I want to know what to focus on. What I need to understand."

The master adjusted his robe. He sipped the water. "First of all, there is no secret. What I will tell you, if you dedicated your life to this search, you would find out for yourself." He reached over dumped out the water, and then refilled the cup from the steaming kettle atop the wood stove. "In thirty years or so," he said, "- with help," and passed the very hot cup to Dashi.

"Is that how long it took you?" asked Dashi moving the hot cup from one hand to the other.

"More or less," said the master, "There are other ways that you could learn much faster. I have found my own, and this I will impart."

Dashi bowed. "Thank you master. What is your teaching?"

"If the cup is too hot to hold, put it down."

Dashi nodded and put the cup on the small woodpile by the woodstove and then sat at attention awaiting his master's words of wisdom. But the master just sat there.

'Ah,' thought Dashi, 'there once was a great master who said – nothing.' He nodded.

"You are nodding. Are you falling asleep?" enquired the master.

Dashi said, "No, master... I understand."

"What do you understand?"

"That it cannot be said in words. Being present. This teaching of yours."

"It isn't mine," shrugged the master.

"No, not yours," said Dashi, "This teaching, the universal teaching of just being."

The master just stared at him, "You are like a kitten tangling yourself up in string. Only *you* manage it without the string."

Dashi slumped in his chair just a tiny bit. "Being present to what is... that's not the teaching?"

The master said, "Everyone knows that. What do you think I've asked you to do? Be in your body. Be present. Don't go off in your thinking so much. But that's only the beginning.

"To see what there is to see, you need be able to experience all the minds freely. If you are not fixated on just one, in your case, thinking mind, then you can easily move amongst them as required."

"How do I move amongst them?" asked Dashi, wondering if that were even the question.

The master said, "Moving is natural. It is not-moving that has been learned. Sticky minds are the difficulty." The master gestured to the cup in the woodpile. "Pick it up."

Dashi took up the hot cup and held it between his burning fingertips. "It's hot," he explained.

"If you grasped the cup and held on with all your might, what would that be like?" asked the master.

"It would be painful," replied Dashi, concerned his master might ask him to do just that.

"Then why do it?" the master asked.

Dashi shook his head, "I wouldn't."

"But you are," insisted the master.

"I'm trying not to," said Dashi shifting the cup back to the other hand for relief.

The master said, "Why listen to me when I tell you to do things that are painful? Don't you have any sense? I will repeat: If the cup is too hot to hold, put it down."

"But you told me to pick it up," said Dashi confused.

The master held up an imaginary bowl in one hand, "You are looking for an answer. If the answer is not in the mind you seek with, you will never find it there. Being stuck in one mind causes unnecessary suffering, like insisting on holding a cup that is too hot to hold." He held up a second imaginary bowl in the other hand, and let the first fall to the floor. "Put that mind down and pick up a different one."

"Ah!" said Dashi, excited, but he misjudged passing the cup back and forth, and it tumbled out of his hands and broke into many many pieces.

V

"Master?" called down Dashi, who was up in the rafters repairing a hole in the roof made by some forest animals looking for a place to live, "How many minds are there?"

"Sixty-four!" the master called back.

"Really?" said Dashi, tying the tarred string to the roof frame.

The master passed him up some thatching. "Of course, twenty-two minds."

"Didn't you say 'sixty-four'?" Dashi asked.

"Yes. Forty-two minds, just like I said, but only twenty-two on festival days."

Dashi pushed the thatch up into the hole. "Master you are having fun with me."

"I am trying to alert you. You are in thinking mind, map making mind, modelling mind."

Dashi put more material in the hole. "Is thinking mind so bad?"

"Not bad," said the master, "except in the sense of a bad habit. Thinking mind is good, when thinking mind is required. You use it too much. You are repairing a roof. Perhaps you should be of a mind that would do a good job, so that we will not have to repair it again."

Dashi finished, backed out of the attic on

his hands and knees, then slowly dangled through the open hatch before letting go and jumping down to the floor. "If I am to move from mind to mind, shouldn't I know what minds I can leap to?"

The master swept the bits of broken thatch out the door. "Monkeys leap from tree to tree. Does it matter what kinds of tree? It matters only that they can get from one to the other. It is the jumping in between that counts. Ask how well you can do that, if you have to ask for a measurement."

The two of them went outside, and both climbed the ladder to work on the weathering coat. The material was put in place, and the master cut the spars with his hook and Dashi hammered them into place.

Dashi said, "Couldn't someone just leap about, so they were always changing their mind? Always changing their point of view so that no one could ever be sure of what they meant?"

"Are you surprised that monkeys are evasive? The kind of person you describe, mostly they are trying to evade themselves. Their claim of perspective is mostly just clambering around in the same tree. The mind that makes maps and models also models and maps the other minds. That is why there are false conditions like: thinking that you are in love, rather than being in love."

"Ah-ha!" said Dashi, "So love is one of the minds?"

The master closed his eyes in silence. When he reopened them he said, "No matter how excellent and detailed the map, it must always leave out detail. Otherwise a map would need to be the size of what it mapped. The question is: what is lost?

"Lists are maps. Naming is not necessarily understanding, it's just putting things in boxes. Any categories I may make to contrast the kinds of minds, is not the experiencing of those minds.

The master pointed to Dashi's hammer. "Thus one hammer is not like another. The craft of cognition is knowing which tool is at hand. It's mastery when that choice becomes intuitive."

Dashi said, "Exactly why I should enumerate them."

"Exactly why you should not," countered the master, "Because in the fixation of thinking about the tools, you lose what that tool actually does, how it is in your hand, and replace it with a conception of what the tool should do. Even just having been in one mind, but commenting from another, requires deep sensitivity in translation."

Dashi mopped his brow, and scratched his head, "Then why do you teach me this? Why give any explanation of minds at all? Just say: 'Do this! - and don't question me.'"

"Because the thinking mind is a curious mind, and it wants to map. Telling you not to think, is to forbid thinking mind. No mind is forbidden. All minds are natural. A mind is a motivation, an energy, a method, an understanding. I am helping you to make a map, that you will know is just a map. Then when you are in thinking mind, you will know you are thinking. You will come to be able to appreciate the limitations of that mind."

"What are the limitations of thinking mind, master?" asked Dashi.

vi

Dashi and the master came to the city on a sunny day to deliver herbs. After they had delivered the last, the master counted the coins. Dashi had not eaten since before the early morning trek down the mountain. He was tired. He tried to relax his mind, to not stay in one state, but his mind returned again and again either to the injustice of his captive brother, or hunger.

"Master, I have tried to do as you ask, but I am still angry," confessed Dashi.

"About what are you angry?" asked the master briefly looking at a street vendor's wire colander.

"The ill treatment of my brother," said Dashi.

"Your anger is understandable," said the master.

Dashi blinked. "But I thought you said I needed to get over my anger?"

"Your outrage, you mean," corrected the master.

"Yes," said Dashi.

"That's not what I said," explained the master, picking up a small strainer, "I said that you needed to understand why you feel the way you do. Why you feel like being hateful. And now you have - tell me the lesson."

Dashi sighed, "I feel angry because of the mind I am in."

"And if you were in a different mind?" prodded the master.

"Then," said Dashi, "I would not feel angry."

"What would you feel then?" Dashi hesitated, so the master went on. "Do you think you'd feel nothing?"

"No," said Dashi.

"Then what?" asked the master, holding up two fingers, bargaining with vendor woman.

Dashi said, "I guess it would depend on what mind I was in."

"Correct," said the master tapping his staff down, "And which mind would you be in?" He held up three fingers.

"The one that is the cure for the mind in which I was stuck," answered Dashi.

The master said, "That is mind as a medicine. But what if there were no longer a problem. If you neither rejected, nor became stuck in any mind? - What mind would you be in then?" He nodded his acceptance to the vendor and gave over some coins.

"Then... any mind would do I suppose,"

said Dashi, following the master back to the street, "The one that I instinctually chose."

The master said, "Exactly. So if you saw ill treatment of someone you loved, what mind would you be in?"

"The one that feels anger, apparently," said Dashi deprecatingly, feeling he was right back where they started.

"Me too," said the master.

vii

At Dashi's request, they entered a busy noodle shop. The tables were rough and well used, but the wide bowls looked new. The scent of the broth was intoxicating. Dashi gazed upon the already eating patron's bowls. Some preferred it simple. Some with extras. A heavy set man right beside Dashi consumed one full of everything. Swimming, glistening jewels of fat twinkled whenever a shaft of sunlight, upon the opening of the shop door, touched the pale liquid's surface.

The owner bowed to the master and asked what the two would like. So hungry, Dashi forgot himself, pointing out what he wanted before the master could speak, and felt the hot flush of embarrassment rise in his cheeks.

The master said, "I will have the same, and he will be paying."

"Very good," said the owner and left to fill their orders.

"... I guess... I didn't realise how hungry I was?" offered Dashi.

The owner soon returned with two steaming bowls of noodles, vegetables, and fragrant spicy exotic dumplings – the broth scented the air with spices from far away lands. The two of them fell to eating with great delight.

Dashi became thoughtful between slurping. "Master, are you not trying to teach me to quiet my mind?"

The master pierced a dumpling. "No... though, that will happen," he said, "I am pulling a donkey out of a ditch."

"You think I'm just being stubborn," said Dashi, after sucking in a noodle.

"That's a mule," said the master, sipping at the broth, "Donkeys feel they have good reason to resist what seems to them unsafe. Because I don't have the strength to make it leave the ditch I have to use persuasion. The donkey, over time, must gain the confidence that it will not be I who leads it into danger."

"Master," said Dashi, slurping the last of his broth, "I regret to say, I don't have the money to pay for this."

"This marvellous soup has restored your memory!" said the master.

viii

The master sat close by as Dashi washed dishes. "Master, when will I be whole?"

"When haven't you been whole?" asked the master.

"You know what I mean, master," said Dashi.

"I do - and I repeat, when haven't you been whole?" said the master.

Dashi said, "By suggestion, you mean I have always been whole. Then why is my mind so disordered?"

"Like the twigs that are found fallen after a storm, is this disorder? The tree remains, but one day a gust will topple it. Where is the disorder?" said the master.

"My desire for order then-" began Dashi.

"Is sticky," said the master, "- in your case. This is a desire of the mapping mind in that it proposes the kind of order you think should be and not the kind that already exists. Truly it is a great consolation that things work themselves out in their own way."

"What way is that?" asked Dashi, scrubbing the bottom of a bowl.

"The way that can be observed and is known by being with it. See how the hot water works in freeing the food from the bowl, with soap it works better. You don't need to understand to see. This is good because the world contains much to see. Understanding a tiny portion is the work of a lifetime. But we can become aware, and then we can see the way it goes."

Dashi rinsed a bowl. "So the disordered way is... my trying to impose order? You mean, by being aware, I'd know what way I go?" said Dashi, "Then I wouldn't be bothered by disorder?"

The master leaned against the counter, "As I have said, a map is useful. You, however, are always checking yours, a constant habit. If you don't want to always be tripping on what's not on your map, you must look up, look about, observe, get another perspective and know things that way. Don't you know already how to wash a bowl? Try just washing one and see if it's the way you remember."

Dashi nodded, listening, and washed a bowl, focusing on how the water slid in a wave as he moved his hands through it, the slipperiness of the dishes in the sink, the roughness of the cloth, the cool of the rinse water, and the clack of it being stacked onto the others "Like that?" he asked.

"Like that," said the master.

ix

Dashi and the master climbed into the forest. It was a hot day. They went up a rough goat path and after a time came to a stream.

There the master gathered water plants. Dashi carefully packed them away. Clouds came up and mist surrounded them. The temperature dropped. Dashi felt damp, and noticed the master's hair was full of droplets.

Resting on a log that was under a gnarled and twisted pine tree, they slowly ate the rice balls they'd prepared in the steaming pot atop the stove, in the morning. Dashi remembered how the glass panes had steamed over with condensation. And how he had written the character for water – its lines dripping and running down the cold morning glass.

"Dashi...," called the master, "for now, be here," he said, and quickly popped into his mouth the last morsel.

x

Dashi swept the floor. His brow was furrowed. The master was seated at the table.

"Master," began Dashi, "where do all the minds come from?"

"Ahh...," said the master nodding wisely and Dashi felt excited that he'd finally asked a really good question. The master put down his cup. "All arises from IT," he said.

"IT?" asked Dashi.

The master sagely nodded.

"What is IT?" asked Dashi.

"No one knows," said the master.

Riddles, thought Dashi. "Why does no one know?"

"Because," said the master, "no one has ever seen IT."

"Why not?"

The master said smiling, "Because IT can't be seen."

"Master am I getting anywhere with this? I mean, should I keep asking or just get on with my sweeping?" said Dashi.

"Just a little more," said the master.

"All right," sighed Dashi, "IT can't be seen... is that because IT sees? - like I do not see my own eyes? Is IT one of the minds?"

"No," said the master, "IT is not *one* of the minds."

"Something other than minds, that cannot be seen by the minds?" reasoned Dashi.

"Yes," said the master confirming.

"Is IT...," said Dashi, "what creates the minds?"

"Exactly so," said the master. "Minds are motivations. They are manifestations of IT."

"Ha," said Dashi, excited that he was finally coming to some answers, "So you cannot see IT except as IT manifests as one of the minds. Seeing with a mind you are looking through IT, but never actually see IT, as such. As you can only be conscious with a mind - each mind has a different opinion of IT."

"Yes. Well done," said the master.

"Master, how should I unify them - all these opinions in front of me?"

"Ahh...," said the master nodding, as he picked up his cup, "By putting them behind you."

Dashi swept the floor.

xi

As Dashi and the master tramped down the mountain to the shack Dashi asked, "Master may I ask you a question?"

"Do," said the master.

"If IT is beyond my knowing, therefore should I not label things as things? Do I just guide myself by intuition, knowing that my minds remember, but I need not do so implicitly with modelling mind?"

The master said, "I remember when you first came seeking to my house. So impertinent and full of self-doubt. You did not notice the way your feet scuffed the ground like a child caught at being naughty. I felt humour and kindness and the feeling one gets on the first step of a journey.

"But as I tell you this story, I am stepping carefully among the roots and do not fall. I follow the narrow winding track and do not get lost. I take care of my old knees and how far they bend. I feel the weight of my stick and my pack, and the damp cool of the air, and the smell of pine and nearby a patch of a wild mint that I will come back for.

"I know there are twelve wild mints, and this one is best for lung complaints. But I know this with sore feet, and the desire for a cup of tea, and the feeling of peace that accompanies me everywhere. I am all here. I am always here.

"If you choose to ignore the body sometimes, then choose it: meditate, explore, think, make up stories. Otherwise, like the centre balance of a scale, be aware of your entire embodiment."

"Because it's grounding?" said Dashi.

"Because it's there," said the master.

xii

Dashi felt the paving stones under his feet. He waded in the throng, following the master in through a maze of walls and houses. The smell of smoke, and cooking, and people living close together in narrow winding ways, filled his breath. Dashi felt a wave of aliveness.

The master had stopped at a door, knocking. A young woman opened the door and bowed to the master, who entered. Dashi followed, ducking under the low doorway, and bowing to the woman who watched him with curiosity. A small warming fire was kept lit in the room's darkened airless oppression. Dashi's eyes adjusted to the gloomy rough plastered room. In the corner of the dim, a bed – there propped up on now faded elegant pillows, was an elderly woman, skin tinged with jaundice. The master bowed and gave her the package of mint he had gathered alone. She made wheezing thanks.

Presently the younger woman appeared carrying a pot of hot water. Dashi was surprised she'd left the room to fetch it. After greeting them she'd apparently faded into the shadows, knowing what the master brought. So quietly, so expertly, he'd not known she'd gone until her return. He sensed she was as attuned to the senses of others as she was to her own. She placed the mint in the pot and billows of scented mist, like the high mountain mist of its origin, cooled the air.

"Dashi," said the master, "we go now." The two left out into the alley, and then back out the long way, crossing the magistrate's courtyard. Dashi glanced at it sideways as he passed.

"Master," said Dashi, "I noticed you did not collect any money from her."

"She taught me the use of many of the herbs I now gather. Including that particular mint," he said, "What else did you notice?"

"That the pillows she had were old but of too high quality for where she now lives."

"Anything else?" said the master.

Dashi said, "Only that the other woman moved in silence, and I felt, she was aware of everyone and everything."

"Did you notice what she put in your pack?" asked the master.

Dashi startled and began to immediately search his pack finding a fountain pen had been carefully wrapped and placed into the pack. "What does it mean?" he said.

"It means that my wife's elder sister is well protected."

"Is that her daughter?" asked Dashi.

"Her grand-daughter," said the master.

"Master, may I ask why her sister does not help her?" said Dashi.

The master said, "I have already explained that, Dashi."

xiii

After a morning of hiking and harvesting they rested. Dashi seated himself, propped comfortably in the shade against the root of a tree, while the master, eyes closed, had stretched himself onto a large, flat, sunny rock for a nap.

"Master, I wish to try to really understand IT..." said Dashi.

"Mystery within mystery... that which cannot be fathomed," said the master smiling, but without opening his eyes.

"...because IT is the source of consciousness," said Dashi.

"Consciousnesses," corrected the master.

"But IT is not conscious itself?" asked Dashi.

"IT is not one of our consciousnesses... Whether IT is conscious..." the master shrugged.

"Then I could come to align my mind with IT?!"

The master popped open one eye and assiduously looked Dashi up and down.

Dashi continued excited, "I mean, if I observe without thought then I should align with IT, yes?"

"No, thinking mind might no longer be

engaged, but another mind would be."

"Right. But what if I could quieten all of them? – What then?" asked Dashi.

The master sighed, "You mean to find the mind under all the other minds?"

Dashi thought a moment. "Yes."

The master rolled onto his side, and propped his head on his bent arm. "This is your assumption," he said, "that because the top of a lake is water, and the middle of the lake is water, that no matter how deep you go, there's just more water.

"Uh... ," said Dashi, "All right, but still I would experience IT."

"I have said, IT is not a consciousness. When you extinguish the last mind, including all your senses: what I have talked to you about are human minds – the ones we can, to some extent, influence – how could you tell you'd come to the undermind, and not just the last mind before you fell unconscious?" asked the master. "You imagine this like blowing out candles in order to see the dark, but it is more like removing your eyes to see what is there when you aren't capable of looking."

"Hmm...," said Dashi considering, furrowing his brow again.

"Let's try a different tack," said the master, "Imagine the minds as all the different parts of a tree: the leaves, the bark, the flowers and so on. For each part we ask, 'What is the seed that created this leaf, this bark, this flower?'

"The answer is always the same seed. But where is that seed? – IT is the seed. A mind is differentiated consciousness – not IT consciousness – excepting that one could consider they may *all*... be IT consciousness."

"A-ha!" said Dashi, "So then you *could* see IT when you are in each of the minds?"

"You are a surprisingly deep, and also mulish thinker, young Dashi," said the master. "But, no, you cannot see IT in the mind you are in. Nor in another mind looking at the first. Not in quiet mind, no mind, joined mind. There is no direct way."

"But then one could..." started Dashi.

Said the master, "When a tree moves, there is wind that moves it, but I cannot see the wind. And I am not trying to be mystical, but the heavens dance and we have minds to see this. Why? Why are things the way they are? Why is there life? Why can we know this?

"Sometimes we can say because of this or that – but at the heart of it... it is unknown." The master slowly gestured at the sky. "Yet deeper still, why is there anything instead of nothing? The source. We are of that. The why of everything is IT. Do you understand?"

"No... that was why I was asking you," said Dashi, resigned, "Master, I am tired of wanting to understand now."

The master clapped his hands. "Finally, some progress."

xiv

Later, standing outside by the fire, the master pointed out the constellations, and they watched for shooting stars.

"Foremost to freeing yourself from the ditch is a sense of humour, and a sense of the sublime," said the master.

Dashi softly brayed in response. "Why those, master?" he said.

Said the master, "If you tend to laugh, if you tend to experience deep wonder: you see when hidden paths appear. Any rut in your mind is jarred by humorous revelation. So you laugh.

"The revelation of sublime mystery, that which remains hidden even in full view, is astonishing and paradoxical. Sometimes so perfectly sublime you have to laugh, and sometimes so funny, it's sublime. These are the junctures between two minds."

"Minds can work together?"

"Absolutely," said the master, "subtle and surprising are their combinations. Haven't I explained that? This is why we seek to free them, so there can arise a greater perspective than what any single mind can create."

"How does the greater perspective happen?" asked Dashi.

"The minds speak," said the master, "They add their views, which are heard by your present point of view, and although it doesn't agree - it trusts, and therefore includes the view in its actions. Thus the minds act in concert."

"Could I experience IT if I were to use all of them at once?"

The master said, "Have you ever wondered why masters are always depicted as white haired, ancient, and stooped?"

Dashi smiled and attended his master with the greatest of care and politeness. "Please, master."

"As close to IT as you will get," sighed the master. "The particular variants of the minds intrinsic to you, Dashi - your character, is the outcome of IT. Every movement you make is grounded in IT. If you could see IT, it would only mean to you as much as your minds take as meaningful. Which if you were unstuck, is the world as you would naturally see it. If you would still chase IT - chase it there in yourself."

"Then it is possible to experience the IT-ness of me. So how do I do that?" asked Dashi.

"By wasting your life staring at your navel!" snapped the master. "If oneness is so perfect, why have so many minds? You are obsessed with trying to stuff the tree back into the seed," the master explained in a firm voice.

"All minds are motivations and stories and language and ways of learning, and so on, because these are the views of each other. This is how they can speak to one another."

"Is it worthwhile for the minds to work together? Of course! This is what stuckness lacks." The master pointed at Dashi's feet. "But if you bound your feet and hands together would they be better at walking or grasping? You desire to understand IT, but do not trust IT. Take heed of the minds you have unless you think you can design a better human."

Dashi bowed, "I'm sorry master, I understand."

"If you would seek IT," said the master, "practice being humbled by IT."

He pointed into the endless black sky. "There is infinity: laugh and wonder!"

XV

The master found Dashi sitting by a stream.

"Where are you?" said the master.

"I am worrying about my brother. How is he? Is he even still alive? I am sorry, master," said Dashi.

"Why are you sorry?"

"Because," Dashi said, "I am stuck in a mind of worry. I am going nowhere. I should change my mind and find a perspective that gives me a solution or resolution."

"Should?" said the master, "You can choose to change. Or maybe you chose to sit by the stream and feel melancholy. It is up to you. And by that I do not mean there is an obvious choice and a foolish one. I mean exactly that you chose your mind and if you wish to worry, why 'should' I be trying to change that?"

"You truly have no opinion?" asked Dashi.

"Very much I have an opinion. Even the mind that just sees life and accepts what is, is an opinion. We haven't talked of good and bad yet have we?"

"No, master," said Dashi.

"Alright then," the master held up one finger. "The discussion of good and bad is either short and simple, or torturous and long," said the master.

"Depending...?"

"Depending on what mind one is inhabiting," said the master.

"I would like the short and simple version, please," said Dashi.

"Just so," said the master, "Imagine a cake, like the one we saw in the town. Do you remember?"

"Yes," said Dashi, sitting forward, "It looked delicious."

"The cake is divided into eight slices, but unevenly. Some slices of the delicious cake are large and others small. You and a group of seven are trying to survive after being shipwrecked. All are very hungry. The group has come upon this cake and are now to divide it amongst you. What way do you propose?"

"Did the cake wash up from the shipwreck?" asked Dashi.

"Probably," said the master.

"It will be soggy with seawater then, and no one will want to eat it."

"It was in a watertight box which you now have opened," sighed the master, "Just consider the question."

Said Dashi confidently, "Obviously we

should recut the cake to divide it equally so that there is no one who feels cheated – thus group harmony would be maintained and we would be able to work best together to help our present circumstance."

"Yes that would be fair and good," said the master, "A clear rational solution. All the young men in your group would be satisfied with that?"

"Yes," said Dashi.

"And would consider that good?" asked the master.

"Of course," replied Dashi.

"And that is how you see the group, young men like yourself, all equally deserving?"

"Indeed, master," said Dashi.

"But I didn't say they were all young men. That was just your assumption. What if I tell you now the group is made up of men and women, young and old, small and large, healthy and sick, some skilled in one way, others in another. Would distributing the cake equally still be consider good by all?"

Dashi began to speak, but halted considering. "That was a trap," said Dashi.

"That was a trap," the master confirmed, smiling, "But answer it anyway. Would not everyone feel that distributing it equally to be fair and therefore good?"

"I suspect they would," sighed Dashi.

"They may say it is the only rational decision. And would that indeed be good?" asked that master.

"No," said Dashi wearily, "because now some need the cake more than others, if they are to all survive. If they need to build a shelter, to catch fish, to collect wood for fire, it would better go to those who can do that."

"Well reasoned, Dashi," said the master.

"Thank you, master."

"But... maybe the situation is hopeless, maybe they are just going to wait to die. What of that?" asked the master.

Dashi said, "I suppose even then, fairness would be to apportion the ration of cake to extend life equally, so they starve at the same time?"

The master watched the stream flow by. "So what is good?" asked the master, "What is fair?"

"I don't know," said Dashi, resting his head on his hand.

"Really?" said the master, in mock surprise, "But I just heard you answer my questions about the fair distribution of rations. And no matter how I changed the scenario you just changed your perspective and always had an answer of what was the good thing to do. Is that not true?"

"Yes," said Dashi.

"So you must know what being fair is," said the master.

"It depends on the situation," said Dashi.

"How many kinds of situations are there?" asked the master.

"Lots," said Dashi.

"An infinite variety?" prompted the master.

"I suppose so. Yes," said Dashi.

"Do you really suppose there are an infinite number of points of view?" asked the master.

"We're now on the torturous and long explanation aren't we?" lamented Dashi.

"Not at all," said the master, "this is the simple version."

xvi

A bee had found its way into the shack in the morning, and Dashi had eased it back outside. Something about it made him think... no, feel, in his body, a sense of a hidden path.

He mused while, again, he swept the floor. He mused while he washed his face. He mused standing stirring the pot. "Master," said Dashi, as he served his master porridge, "If the minds were like petals or a wheel... and I was stuck on one petal, then I would see each of the other petals from that perspective, and might think that I was changing my perspective, but really I wouldn't be - not unless I fly to the other petals. That's being stuck."

"In the shelf under the bed, behind the herb box, is a jar of honey," said the master.

xvii

In the dark, the warmth emanating from the stove onto Dashi's face was like sunshine. The pad was thin but without lumps, the blanket of adequate length if turned the right way. Dashi stared into the night. There was no moon. There was no wind outside. The master made no sound. The world, like the embers in the stove, silent, crept along. The hum of being was in his mind, a hot summer wind, that gusts here and there but doesn't know quite where to go. Dashi let his senses go out into the world.

His mind settled in the tops of the trees all around them. It drifted down across the rooftops in the town. Dashi stood in the square outside the magistrate's palace in the blue darkness and stared at its inky walls. He placed his hands against the giant double door, felt the large embossed symbols of office, noticed their contours. Noticed that the indent that came down was such that rain would be able to gather there. He put his finger into the space.

"Magistrate concerned about appearances," he said in his sleep, before drifting into deeper slumber.

The master was very pleased.

xviii

One day Dashi was washing the clothes. The water was becoming cold and the plant soap less sudsy as he scrubbed. Dashi twisted and wrung out another shirt.

"Laundry is endless," he thought. Then he thought about all the people doing their laundry: here in town and in the province, in the capitol, in far away lands. All the different clothing, the different tubs, the different people. Laundry, everyday, as far into the future as he could imagine, and as far into the past: endless, infinite laundry.

The ridiculous idea made Dashi smile. He laughed.

xix

A runner came early one day and delivered a letter. The master read it and went inside, telling the runner to wait. Dashi was still asleep by the stove. The master placed the letter on the table and finding paper and pen wrote a reply which he sent back with the boy. Dashi awoke.

"Good morning," said the master.

"Good morning, master," said Dashi yawning, "Who was that?

"I have received word about your brother," said the master pushing the letter towards Dashi.

Dashi looked at it and said, "I do not understand that character." He pointed.

"Oh," the master said taking the letter. "Let me then. It says that your brother is being sequestered... meaning he is being hidden, and is no longer in the main jail. We assume because of his political views."

"Ah... they told you about that," said Dashi.

"I knew about your brother before you climbed the mountain to see me," said the master.

"Then you agree with what he stands for?" asked Dashi.

The master put the letter down on the table. "No, I did not say that."

"But the freedom of the people..." started Dashi.

"Yes, is very laudable and," said the master, "also theoretical." The master stood up. "You think I am teaching you a different way of looking at things for no reason? Your brother and his followers see things one way, and the magistracy another. You came to me because you had doubt," said the master. "Lucky you. Your brother is no doubt in a dungeon."

"What should I do master?" asked Dashi.

"That's up to you," said the master standing, gazing out the window his back to Dashi. "There is no right answer. If you decide what I decide that only means we decide the same thing. The actual answer is unimportant, it is how you proceed with answering that is crucial," he said, "My little teaching is over. You understand all you need to."

Dashi thought for a moment, "Master, what will you do?"

"I am waiting," said the master.

"Then I will wait too," said Dashi.

The master said, "Ah... but what will you be waiting for?"

"I will be waiting for someone wiser than me to stop waiting," said Dashi.

XX

"Master, how do you choose which mind to be in?" asked Dashi, leaning against the tree by the sunny reedy stream where it fed into the river

The master said, "I have told you," as he lay still on the bank, with his right arm lying in the water.

Dashi said, "Would you please tell me again?"

"Do not avoid any mind Dashi. And do not stay in any mind too long. That is the same thing – you stay too long because you are avoiding another. No grasping. No rejecting. Flow from one to the next." A good size fish came closer but then darted away.

"Ah..." said Dashi, rather like the way the master would have, holding up one finger. "But, how do you choose?"

The master only moved an eyebrow, eyeing another fish that came to the edge to rub its belly on the rocks. "You don't. You clear the way so that anything may happen. Then you let it happen."

"Like insight?" said Dashi.

"Indeed," said the master, "That is one thing." With that the master hooked his arm up quickly tossing the fish out of the water.

Dashi caught the flopping fish and put it in the bag with the other.

"So you remain passive?" asked Dashi.

"There is no passivity. The cycle of things brings opportunity. The minds respond, grow, take advantage... given what you are," said the master.

"What I am?" asked Dashi.

"That you are Dashi and will always be that. The Dashi of the high road, Dashi of the low road. The form of IT you are. Integrated or disintegrated, your successes and failures will be yours. If you become wise, you will be wise in your own way, just as you will be foolish to your own propensity," said the master, eyeing another fish.

"Why is that?" said Dashi.

The fish swam away. "Hmm...? Oh... You, me, everyone, has inclinations to some minds over others. You like these, I like those, usually because they are stronger. My former wife for example is a talented musician," said the master, "If you overlook the stuck notes... Minds can have near bottomless depth."

"By depth you mean a mind-" started Dashi.

"I mean the refinement of its desires. Plus the coordination with the other minds, just as one does with other people. That's why I told you, seek those who like what you do. Also they will encounter similar difficulties, and solutions, so depth can be created together."

"When did you say that?" asked Dashi.

"When we first met," answered the master. "I do hope you are paying attention."

"Ah... Of course," said Dashi, "Value what others value."

"No, no," said the master. "Find those who like you for who you are and what you like. Of course, avoid those who make gods of whatever values they idealise, or demonise the slightest disagreement. Sadly, we, the people have a tendency to be attracted to those exhibiting a uniform stuckness. It makes them seem so confident."

"The people... What of the people?" said Dashi. "...their tendency?"

The master sat up on the bank and rolled down his sleeve on his cold wet arm. "The people, eh?" The master took off his shoes and picking up his staff, waded to the other side of the stream. There he stood up upon a rock, his arms wide, his staff raised, and spoke in a great voice. "This is a question that is very important, but also very dangerous. The understanding of this grants to one great power!"

Then arms down, and humbly leaning upon his staff, his voice lowered to normal. "But... I counsel the path of true freedom."

Dashi nodded, "For the people. Yes, I understand."

"No, for you," said the master, pointing at Dashi. "Those who wield power become enmeshed in politics. That is a life of a slave that mistakes itself a master. Yes?"

"Yes, master," said Dashi.

"Now, your question," said the master, getting down off the rock, and then sitting upon it. "The propensity of average people is for leveraging. Do the minimum and get the maximum. Leveraging mind is the stuck form of creative mind. Why is this?"

Dashi answered, "By being used too much."

"Yes," said the master. "They assess everything in this way: What is its advantage to me? This tree, this rock, what does it get me? They leverage possessions, and money, and beauty and skill. They leverage the world, and each other, and themselves. Why are they stuck?"

"Because there is a mind that they are avoiding," said Dashi.

"True," said the master, "Also they have

been told by their elders that this is a valuable mind... along with mapping mind, authority mind, and so forth. If you have a capable mind: leverage it. Leveraging is a safe place to hide, but from what?"

"Wait, master," said Dashi, "Are you saying some minds are stronger in some people, and that this makes for their preference of mind – or that we are trained into them?"

"Both," said the master. "Society has work to do, so indulges their favourites."

"Does society have a mind?" asked Dashi.

"No," said the master, "but depending on what any society needs (or thinks it does) it will encourage some minds, and ignore others. Like dividing a cake, circumstances change, so needs change, and then the society changes because different minds are now favoured."

"So presently people need to leverage," said Dashi.

"They need to be creative," corrected the master. "It is the over emphasis. Having to utilise everything makes that mind sticky. So, again, what are they hiding from?"

"True freedom?"

"Indeed," said the master. "You are repeating my words back to me very well. What then is true freedom?"

"I have no idea," said Dashi.

The master sighed, "I know," The corner of his mouth turning up. "Why don't we use thinking mind?" he said.

Dashi leaned hard against the tree and thought.

"Well..." he began, palms up, "if leveraging mind is a place to hide - they feel safe there. It hides them from the mind they don't like. Is that right?"

"It is," said the master, "Continue."

Dashi said, "But the hidden mind hasn't gone away, so it must mean it is hard to see from that one."

"Yes," said the master.

"It's probably right beside them," said Dashi.

The master tilted his head. "Remarkably astute. Continue."

Dashi touched his chin. "All the other minds tell the stuck mind how to become unstuck... Ah! - the stuck mind understands the hidden mind the least - it's the one."

"What do you mean?" asked the master.

"It, what the hidden mind says seems... wrong to the stuck mind," said Dashi.

"Wrong?" said the master.

"Wrong... like the opposite of what it wants... ahhh," nodded Dashi. "That makes sense."

"Give an example," said the master.

"Creative mind tries to utilise things. To make things happen, figure it out, find the answer. But just as you've said – it is over-emphasised," said Dashi, "It is looking at everything for advantage. It wants to utilise everything."

"Opportunistic," said the master.

Dashi nodded. "Yes, I see that. Creative mind tries to create freedom, but it can't. It has gone too far, making a false god of itself, and a demon of the true freedom mind – that it now despises."

"So what is true freedom, Dashi?"

Dashi was silent and then said, "I still don't know. But the mind that does know is the one the stuck mind is least likely to listen to."

The master nodded. "Consider," said the master, "By freedom most people seek the answer to the easy life. By which they really mean the leveraged life. This is not what is meant by true freedom."

"You mean they are lazy."

"I mean most people's efforts are very low, and they do not understand the bind they put themselves in," said the master.

Dashi said, "By being stuck."

"Stuck, indeed," repeated the master. "In rejecting a mind, they retreat to another that cannot fathom the first. However the rejected mind's concern is still valid. Whatever it is telling them, they are now either ignorant or slanderous, or both. The easy freedom they covet is this state of ignorance."

"Sad," said Dashi.

The master smiled. "That is the sign of a good heart," he said.

"What is?" asked Dashi.

"Never mind," said the master, and continued, "If there is a way to get someone else to do it, to make a device that relieves them of the effort, or to take a slave – they will prefer it. They never think it might be they who becomes the slave."

"Their freedom is short sighted," said Dashi.

The master leaned forward, "If you do not free people's minds, there is no true freedom, only leveraging. Eventually they will leverage for things contradictory to their survival."

"Yes... short sighted," restated Dashi, nodding. "How is this then resolved?"

The master laughed. "It is resolved when the natural consequences of holding contradictory values eventually eliminates whatever false freedom they created and it all comes crashing down on their heads."

"All because they won't change their mind," said Dashi.

"Exactly," said the master, "So, what is it?"

"What's what?" replied Dashi.

"True freedom..." said the master.

"Can't you just tell me?" asked Dashi.

"So you can remember?" asked the master.

"Yes, master."

"You are very good at that," said the master.

"Thank you, master," said Dashi.

"That might not have been a compliment," said the master.

"Oh," said Dashi.

"It is simple to see what is present, far more difficult to see what is not," said the master, "True freedom comes from being willing to see that which is not present."

"I understand, master," said Dashi, "No, I lie – I have no idea. What is the answer?"

The master folded his robe across himself as he did when he was expecting to sit a while. "Do you not? They leverage instead of creating – because they avoid what specifically, Dashi?" asked the master.

"I don't know," said Dashi.

"You do know," said the master, "And what is more, this you will find on your own. My teaching is over. Answer this yourself."

xxi

Dashi looked down, looked within. He was still half standing, leaning against the same tree – but everything was different. He didn't think he knew, but the master had confidence in him. If that didn't make Dashi feel confident, then at least it made him willing to try. "Yes, master, I will answer this," he said, looking up. "But may I still ask questions?"

"The sun and the moon would cease in their path before that could ever be," replied the master.

Dashi squinted his eyes, putting on his thinking mind. He wore it now with what he felt was a sense of lightness, in that he might need change to another mind to solve this riddle. He reasoned that the people used their creative minds to bend things to themselves, and that meant what...? That they were using their wills. Always being willful meant... that they were never unwillful. What is unwillfulness?

"Is this about being willful?" asked Dashi.

"The will of the people is weak because they use it frivolously," replied the master.

"Too much," said Dashi.

"Too much," the master confirmed.

"Like their creativity used too much becomes leveraging."

"Just so," said the master.

"This has the same root – that which is rejected," said Dashi.

"Indeed," said the master, "The whole fabric of the self is warped by willful ignorance. I reveal to you now that there is no reason one can't can be stuck in several minds at once."

A bottomless chasm opened before Dashi's feet. "Then, how do I know I'm even chasing the right mind to be free?" asked Dashi.

"You don't," said the master, "However my questions are guiding you, because I do."

Dashi thought then about the master's questions. He said, "You have told me about their leveraging and not their over use of their will, even though they have the same root. Is this your guidance?"

"Yes," said the master, and leaned on his staff.

Dashi looked up. "If you had spoken of the will then I should have said giving up... but leveraging, creating..."

"Is giving up a mind?" said the master. "Of what use to our ancestors was giving up mind?"

Dashi considered. "I can not think of a

use."

"Nor I," said the master, "Like giving up in a way, but not giving up."

"You counsel true freedom," said Dashi.

"I do."

"This is freedom of the minds then," Dashi stated.

"It is," confirmed the master.

"To free the people is to free their minds," said Dashi.

Said the master, "I have already stated as much."

"Yes, master you have," said Dashi. No solution was coming to him. "But not to be free from their minds."

"No," said the master.

Dashi looked down at the bag with the two plump dead fish. "Master, may I sit under the tree?"

"I have made myself comfortable. You may do likewise."

Dashi sat down under the tree.

At this, the master stood. "I am going home," said the master. "You stay here." The master crossed the stream to Dashi's side and put on his shoes. "When you are hungry, and the sun has set, come and eat, then sleep. But return here tomorrow at sunrise, and sit. Unless you ask me a question, I will remain silent."

The master took the bag with the freshly caught fish, and walked down the mountain, leaving Dashi, pondering, beneath the twisting tree, where the master and he had first met.

xxii

The sun was sitting below the horizon. Dashi was sitting below the tree in thought.

"The answer is nothing that I can leverage," he thought. "Therefore I cannot find this through thinking. I cannot find this through acting. I cannot find this through reasoning. Trying to turn any tool to my advantage is to my disadvantage.

"But it is not just giving up because that is not a mind. There is no path in that. It's just an escape. Trying to escape from one's minds is itself the problem of stuckness. Therefore it is a mind, but one that I cannot see from leveraging. A mind that leveraging mind can't understand. One that seems to it, wrong."

Dashi repeated these ideas until his thinking mind had the territory mapped. He knew that what he sought was not on the map itself but in the territory. And that he'd narrow it to a specific area.

"Leveraging mind is always trying to change things. To escape from what is to something else. But not just letting things be? Is it indifferent mind? Is indifferent mind a mind our ancestors would have needed?

"What is the mind that does not try to take advantage, nor tries to escape, nor is indifferent, but our ancestor would have needed?"

"Free the minds."

"Ah," thought Dashi, "to move freely between all minds doesn't happen if this mind is rejected." And then, "This mind is the answer to being able to move in and out of all minds. It is necessary for free minds." Dashi nodded, indeed he thought this was the key insight.

The master knew he had to get to it himself. Not to think it, not to reason it, but to move to this mind. To see with this mind. And all the minds Dashi knew would not help him. But the master said he knew it. But he did not know that he knew it. He held it in his hand but did not see it. Obviously he was as close as he'd ever be, and yet he was missing it. Dashi felt frustrated and foolish. And hungry.

The tree stood alone below the darkening, star dusted sky.

xxiii

Dashi ate his dinner in quiet contemplation. The master did not speak.

xxiv

While sitting beneath the twisted tree, in front of Dashi a fish swam by in the stream. He wondered if this was a sign. He realised this was tying to create an answer. Force one by his will.

It wasn't the what, he realised, it was how he saw. It was inside him. The whole world was Dashi's world. The world as it appeared to him. This is why this was so hard to see, it was invisible to the viewer though it was all around. "What is water to a fish?" he thought.

He looked at the fish who pecked at the surface of the water.

Dashi had spent a great deal of time walking back and forth rather than sitting under the tree as the master had said.

One day the master had caught him pacing – the master, standing off to one side silently, for Dashi didn't know how long before he'd noticed him.

"Master, my legs cramp," said Dashi, abashed, "Is it all right that I can get up once in a while?"

The master smirked. "What do you think? Does it matter to the answer what position your body is in?"

"I suppose not," said Dashi.

"Suppose?" repeated the master.

Dashi nodded. "Yes, I suppose it doesn't matter at all."

The master was silent a moment and then again said, "Suppose?"

Dashi stood tall. "Master, it doesn't matter. I could hang upside-down in the tree and this would make no difference."

From that point on Dashi paced and sat and leaned against the trunk and sat with his feet in the stream and lay on the ground. He wandered around the tree. Occasionally he would go across the stream and sit on the rock and look at the tree hoping the perspective might trigger a different way of seeing. He threw rocks in the river.

Dashi's thoughts drifted to thinking about the people seeing differently, and how that could be done, but only as conjecture as he didn't even yet know what way they would need to see. He acknowledged the thought, and his intention, and then focused on trying to see what wasn't there.

"Master," he asked when they were lying down to sleep, "have I ever been in this mind before?"

"Yes," said the master.

"Recently?" asked Dashi.

"Yes," replied the master.

"Have I used this mind today, master?" he asked.

"Undoubtably," said the master with mirth in his voice.

"Master, this is like a riddle where once I see the answer it will be obvious?" said Dashi.

"Naturally."

"Master it is frustrating," said Dashi.

"You *feel* frustrated," corrected the master, "If you cannot see the solution..."

"...try another mind. That is what I am trying to do," said Dashi.

"Exactly the problem. You are trying," said the master.

"Aagh..." said Dashi, and turned over to sleep.

XXV

He sat on the boulder. Dashi had supposed he shouldn't think, but then supposed that thinking, or any other of the minds, that he might enter... well he supposed they were just as much not the mind that he sought and he supposed he might as well then...

Dashi couldn't remember quite how that thought began or quite where it was going, so he started a new one.

"This mind doesn't try... moves between minds...does this without doing. How do you do without doing? Come on Dashi, work it out."

"It doesn't do... it lets something else do," said a mind.

"Oh... Not letting go - It's the gatekeeper... it doesn't make anything do, it's only the space in which they act."

"Ah..." thought Dashi, "I'm getting somewhere," he encouraged himself. "I'm zeroing in on some tiny portion of the map. I've almost got it."

"Invisible to leveraging," said a mind.

He thought and he thought. He tried it this way and that. But every corridor of thought that seemed so promising yielded just doors that led to other corridors. The sun rose high and continued marching, arching slowly from east towards the western horizon. It saw Dashi lie in the grass, perch on the branch, wade in the stream, throw pebbles into the river.

Dashi hung upside-down from the lowest strong branch of the tree. "Aagh..." he realised in disgust, "I'm trying to make it happen - I'm trying to think it out even though I know I can't think it out by thinking but I think if I'm just clever and think a little more I'll think of the way to think my way there.

"I can't help myself. I just keep thinking. This isn't working! I'm going in stupid circles-"

"- trying to leverage."

There was a silence while he let that realisation swallow itself.

"Ohhh... Shit." Dashi sank into himself, exhaling, giving up. He couldn't get there from here.

"I'm a leverager," Dashi denounced. And here came the further admission to himself, that, in fact, he leveraged all the time. The guilt of self denunciation is a poignant sorrow.

"Damn..."

Dashi breathed in, begging his fire breath

to save him. The blood running to his head, making it begin to pound, made its intensity, made his bearing down all the more potent. The angry recrimination, burning it, the black charcoal crust surrounding the white hot core, breaking away. He burned away having to make it happen.

He intoned to himself, "I know I believe that I have to work it out - it's my ego - I did this myself - It's my addiction to making it happen - Leveraging is my trying - It is not the path to true freedom - Not trying - Not even wanting - Not even wishing - Nor hoping it should be the way I want - I'm sorry..."

"..."

Dashi laughed. He nearly fell out of the tree. And then - he fell out of the tree. Dashi ran down the mountain side laughing. He ran and avoided the roots, and rocks, and the day was bright and the sky was flecked with tiny clouds, and his breathing was clear and his feet fell heavy, and he almost lost his shoe, and then he lost his shoe, so he went back and got it, and he ran all the way to the shack and the master stood outside smoking a pipe, watching as he approached.

"Master," asked Dashi, panting "Your making me go through the process of searching for an answer myself, and not just receiving it, imply the answer I seek?"

"You're asking?" said the master, puffing on his pipe.

"I assert it," said Dashi.

The master took the pipe out of his mouth, "I agree," said the master smiling.

"Master, the answer is trust," said Dashi.

III

The Magistrate

The narrow alleyway twisted back and forth until it split, at the point of which was a herbalist shop. Inside, it was all dark wood, walls lined with drawers of every size, labeled and numbered. The herbalist measured out the herbs the master had brought on an iron scale, and the herbalist and the master chatted business.

Dashi looked at the names on the herb drawers: Self-Reliant Existence, Awesome Spiritual Immortal, Thousand Years of Health. They sounded so good he wondered if he needed any. He didn't think so.

He watched the stream of soot climb out of the oil lamp and examined the dark stain on the ceiling. The smell was indescribably complex: woods and waxes, herbs and hides, root and fungus, mixed in the caldron of air – heated by candle and customer, stirred by entrances and exits, fermenting. A compounded essence of healing substance.

Its scents had baked themselves into the walls for how ever long the shop had been here, and now released themselves in minute measure, adding hundred year old cures to each and every lungful. One didn't need to consume any of the preparations, merely standing in the whirl of the shop's medicinal scent was enough to cure most people of every illness. Indeed Dashi felt more well and calm than he'd felt for years.

The master and the shop owner were speaking now in low tones bent towards each other. Dashi could see they spoke of something that was serious. He did not think about what it might be, only that the master would tell him when and if he felt it was time to do so. Dashi realised just how much of his thoughts went to things that he could not change, at least immediately. The fate of the people, this and that.

In finding trusting mind, he trusted that the mind that arose was fine, and when another replaced it, that too was fine. Saying yes to yourself, saying yes to every mind, even to the minds that said no.

Hear yourself out, and find clarity. Freedom of mind is letting every mind speak. The alternative, demonisation, the distrust of our very minds, creates the very terrors which we seek to avoid.

"You seem pleased with yourself," said the master who was standing beside Dashi.

Surprised, Dashi laughed, "I was just musing," he said, "Yes, you're right I do feel pleased with myself."

"It isn't vain obsession though," suggested the master.

"Just so," said Dashi, and they laughed.

"Let us go," said the master and they walked out into the lane. Dashi noticed the sky had overcast while they were inside. He went to comment on the weather but followed the master's gaze to a figure moving away from them.

"He saw us," said the master, "We must go."

"Master," said Dashi, "who was that?"

"Someone I do not wish to speak of within earshot of anyone other than a group of trees," said the master and they continued walking. Quickly they picked their way through the streets and in no time they were outside the walls, past the shanty hovels of Dashi's people and tramping down dirt paths rucked with long wheel impressions in the now dry mud.

Only after they had made the journey past the enclosing buildings, stately homes, city gate, surrounding hovels and had once again gained the safety of the mountain trees did the master stop and turn to Dashi. "That man knows me. He was the secretary of the local Magistrate."

"Was?" said Dashi.

"You may have noted the loss of one ear," said the master, "He has a habit of listening to things he ought not to hear and then relating them to others to ingratiate himself. This brought about his diminishment to a lowly jail guard.

"However, I understand that he enjoys the company of other men's wives. Further that in this capacity has been of some service, and is now head jailor and torturer. But his position is precarious and his mistress fickle.

"I suspect he wishes to further ingratiate himself to her. It appears he has learned little."

"By reporting seeing you?" asked Dashi.

"Seeing us," said the master, "Although he does not know you. Being the jailor he will have seen your brother, and I know the two of you bear a resemblance. He will report that you and I are in league."

"I would hardly call us in league with each other," said Dashi.

"Not the way he will tell it," said the master, "Come."

"Dashi," said the master, lying on his back in the high meadow, "I suspect changes are moving towards us that will end our time on the mountain."

"Yes, master, I will move on then," said Dashi.

The master put his hand on Dashi's shoulder, "But that change has not happened yet," said the master, "Watch the clouds."

The sky was dashed with the best kind of big fluffy clouds, with little fast ones skittering beneath them and high long streams of cloud far above.

"Master," said Dashi, "Can you read the future in the clouds?"

"Yes, of course," said the master, pointing to the largest cloud nearby, "First there is something that becomes big and important, and then it either changes form - dissipates - or there are tears as it exhausts itself. That is the future." The master turned his head, "And how is that like the minds Dashi?"

"I thought your teaching was over," commented Dashi.

"O yes, teaching ends, but not learning," said the master, plucking a tiny, white, bitter flower, and promptly eating it.

"Yes, master," said Dashi, "I understand."

The master smiled, "If I'm speaking, you're learning."

They'd been to town and took care not to be seen, or recognised if they were seen, by acquiring different clothing.

The rain drizzled. Up the mountain path the trees swept from side to side slowly. Brown leaves sat sodden before them, as the two climbed back to the shack.

When they reached the shack the master poured water on his mud splattered shoes, putting them up to dry and he did so also for Dashi sitting on the bench, back against the shack wall, staring out upon the blowing tree tops. The master busied himself making fire, and when that was done brought Dashi inside and took his cloak. The master turned down his own bed and bade Dashi, weary and numb, get in. Then the master pulled the blanket over Dashi's shoulders.

The master lit a small candle for Dashi's brother. He made himself some tea and sat at the table watching the slow snaking steam rise, its grey against the bluing light as night darkened the world, with only the single eye of red flame inside the stove visible.

The day was bright and cool. The onion leaves had turned brown and fallen over. It was time to harvest. Dashi bent over and pulled one onion after another and placed them into the basket beside him.

"Master, there is something I have to tell you," said Dashi pausing his toil, "My brother wasn't arrested for just poaching a deer. I lied." There was silence.

"I know," said the master.

"Are you angry?"

"Rarely," said the master not even bothering to look up from pulling a particularly fat onion from the earth. "Are you?"

Dashi plunked another onion into the basket, "Yes, master, I find I am."

"Did I ever tell you about stuck mind?" joked the master.

"Little else," said Dashi.

"Then tell me about anger," said the master.

Dashi looked deep into the dirty onion he'd just pulled from the earth, "Anger is natural. It is a reaction from a mind," Dashi said, "An ancient mind. It is fighting mind, and defending mind," he added, "It is also the mind that nurses grudges."

"Grudging mind is different, but go on. Is it trusting?" asked the master.

"No. It defends itself. It closes itself off for survival," said Dashi.

"And this is what you feel?" asked the master.

"Yes," said Dashi, "My brother is dead. I know I cannot retrieve him. To avenge him is merely to die. The magistrate is powerful. So I see my brother as a martyr." He added the onion to the basket. "I know that the magistrate sees things differently." Dashi looked up at the sky, "But I sit with my anger... and I don't know how to proceed. Do I follow the flow of my anger which is deep within me, or seek to divert it with another mind."

"You are slipping between minds even as we speak," said the master, "Why else talk of the futility of force? Or the irrevocability of death and time?"

"I do well?" asked Dashi, "Even bearing a grudge?"

"Yes," said the master.

Dashi looked at the master, having seated himself among the onions, "But is it enough?"

"Here is my teaching: even if the door is open wide, any mind you cannot leave: is a cell. – How can you tell? Leave your anger, and come back to it. Leave it again, and come back again. You feel hurt. But this is nothing. If you cannot escape a mind, even if only briefly out of its grip, then you are a prisoner, and your own jailor. To become unstuck we merely require trust enough to move to the mind that cures it. "

Dashi said, "Then what mind cures this?"

"You know it," said the master and returned to the picking of onions. "You dream of it. But I council to first find your revolution within.

"After trust, after we no longer insist that the world *must* be the way we want it to be, we need to deal with the world, which is still difficult, without succumbing to fear. Thus we cleanse ourselves of the ghosts of habits that caused one to fearfully latch onto the ideal essence in the first place. The work of becoming unsticky becomes natural, effortless, as the minds begin to repair themselves. After that, we welcome our renewed character – which will surprise you."

The master put his hand on Dashi's

shoulder, "I have shown you how to grieve - but there is more to the practice. When you breathe in, know that this is your life, and this may even be your very last breath. Therefore treat the incoming breath with the gratitude it deserves. Then breathe out. Gratitude, grief, gratitude, grief. Whatever you are experiencing, your breath has brought you here.

"Life is sweet, and if you practice, so too can, a little, be death." The basket full to overflowing, the master stood and took them to cure beneath the shading eaves.

"My brother was no innocent," Dashi thought to himself, "But still, I loved him." Dashi let the tears come as he gathered onions, unaware a dragonfly had settled upon his back.

"I refuse to be a victim," he thought, breathing in the cool, alive, fragrant mountain air, and exhaling - concentrating the stream of his breath into the hot coal of his grief.

Dashi stoked the fire.
"You will make the fire too hot if you use so much wood," said the master.

Dashi stopped. "Sorry, master. My mind is elsewhere."

"Where are you? What are you thinking?" asked the master.

"The magistrate," said Dashi, "he must be removed."

The master nodded, "Every four years," he said.

"I mean now," said Dashi, "It's not good to have him there."

"I do not understand what you mean," said the master.

Dashi furrowed his brow. "I mean," he said, "he's the enemy of the people. He's not good. He's a monster."

The master shook his head. "Dashi," he said, "this is my left hand." The master held out his left hand. "And this is my right hand." The master held out his right hand. "Agreed?"

"Yes, master, of course," said Dashi.

"Now," said the master, "This is my left hand," and again he held out his left hand. "And this is not my left hand." And once again he held out his right hand. "Agreed?"

"Yes, it is just the same as before," said Dashi.

"Is it?" said the master, who took a stick of firewood from the pile. "This is not my left hand," said the master. He pointed to the table, "This is also not my left hand." The master reached out and took Dashi's left hand in his, "This also is not my left hand," said the master. "'Not good,' informally, is fine. You expect me to intuit what you mean. But as a description such as you have made, it is a problem."

The master smiled, squinting his eyes, "It's not good."

"Because I am not being specific," said Dashi.

"Because you use a negative in place of a positive without knowing the trap," said the master, pointing, "Look here - Dashi, step three steps forward, and then three steps back."

Dashi did as he asked.

"In this you think back is the same as backwards, but that is just the way you are facing. This time start by taking three steps backwards."

And Dashi did so.

The master said, "Now take three steps back."

And Dashi returned forward to the spot where he began.

"You see?" said the master, "Three this way, and then three in return, regardless of direction. Positive three steps, and then negative three steps. Agreed?"

"Yes, master," said Dashi who was wondering where the master was going with this.

"Now, Dashi," said the master, "Take three steps back."

Dashi hesitated and then took a step backward.

"No," said the master immediately, "That is backward. I said, take three steps back. Take three negative steps."

Dashi thought a moment, "Master there is no way to return three steps, before I take them in the first place."

"Exactly," said the master, "You think because you have an idea of what the good is you know what not good is. Not good is negative good.

"Like, not my left hand. It is just a place holder: not here, not right, not yellow, not a dog. It is a mistake to think of it as defining something. Whatever the magistrate may be, a not-something is pointless as taking three negative steps. When you define, consider the use of positives."

"I stand corrected. The magistrate is a tyrant," said Dashi.

"Much better," said the master.

"Thank you," said Dashi who felt the master was being overly picky.

The master eyed Dashi, who suspected some of his thoughts were showing. "Why do you think I focus on this?" asked the master.

"So that I say what I mean," replied Dashi.

"Good answer," replied the master.

"Thank you, master."

"What you mean is you prefer things one way. So do I. And so does the magistrate. This does not make us the anti-you. Instead of a gradation, as fine as you wish to make, between limits, these extreme categories are what makes for stuckness.

"Stuck mind puts on airs and deigns to speak for IT. An authoritarian play of shadow and light." The master held up his left hand. "Hand and anti-hand – in other words: the enemy," said the master, "If a mind insists its want *must* be the only truth, then every other point of view is automatically against that truth. The ideal good gives birth to monsters. Do you understand?"

"But, he is my enemy," professed Dashi.

"That's a no, then," said the master.

"He is a murderer, and a tyrant. He wishes to make everyone his victim, I understand this about him."

"No, I can guarantee that you do not understand the minds of the magistrate," said the master, "As for being a victim, if you are setting yourself on not being one, I will point out that insistence is not trust. Be confident in your minds. They are not as fragile as you suspect. This is then the extreme: the good and the anti-good. The good you imagine as being upheld by yourself, of course. The anti-good is from others. If you want to end up hating everything and everyone, this is a *good* way to go."

"Can I not be angry?" asked Dashi.

"Hate is not anger," said the master, "And it also is not trust. There are people who want other things than you do, and may oppose you. They are just other people. A pig that eats your food is hungry, not an enemy. Nor is the wolf at the door.

"To the trusting mind there are no forbidden thoughts. But there is an understanding of the grip of them. Different in kind are: exemplary and unwanted, from gods and devils. Enemies are devils. Therefore you hate. It wouldn't matter if the magistrate was the greatest of musicians, you'd hate the music on principle."

"So I should not try to change things in the world?" demanded Dashi.

"Not with that attitude," said the master,

"Everything will just go sideways."

"Sorry, master," said Dashi, "I feel pulled apart."

"Perfect cherished notions are destructive because they are addictive. This is how stuckness happens. The other minds' voices are silenced. Their comments are not just dissent, but heresy. Temper extremes. This is what I teach.

"And, I know if I would teach, a student must not put me on a pedestal that they cannot themselves climb. Vast temples, golden thrones, and flowing robes make it much harder to see clearly. Temple bells and silence deafen one to the simplicity of the learning. Fellow acolytes' snores rankle your patience because they divert you from the vision of perfection you aim at – making you lie awake, scheming how to attain it. Luckily, you listen to me snore – sleeping on the floor of some strange old man living in a shack.

"This thing that you insist should be. Maybe it will be and maybe it won't. But if you can accept what you are, you can be at peace."

"Again, you mean I should do nothing," said Dashi.

"Again, I counsel to know yourself," said the master.

Again the weather was grey. A light mist stuck to the forest in places as they climbed windingly upward among gnarled wind-shaped twisted trees, Dashi following the master.

"Come on, keep up," encouraged the master, "We're almost there."

Dashi doubled his efforts and as they came around the top of a rise he saw the cave. Just then it began to rain and the two sought shelter in its mouth.

"That's why I had you carry all those sticks on your back," said the master. And Dashi took the load he'd quite forgotten he carried and laid the kindling down with an echoing clatter at the front of the cave. Where upon the master began stacking it for a fire.

Dashi had noted before how deftly the old man made fire, but had never watched closely enough to see him do it. Did he have a flint? For soon enough the fire was burning and the master was busying himself with a flat rock which he pushed into the fire and a metal pot for tea he put upon it. The full skin hanging from the master's shoulder he took off and poured into the pot. The scent of herbs began to fill the cave.

Dashi looked into the depths of the cave, "Are you sure no one is at home?"

"I'm sure," said the master who was fanning the dense steam that came from the pot. "Now," he said presently, "Up 'til today I have never spoken with you of politics. Would you like to know my mind?"

Dashi nodded, "Yes, master. Very much I wish to understand your view."

"All right," said the master, "Then I will tell you the story of Jade Mountain." Dashi settled in for the tale. "Once, in a distant land, there lived a Monkey King. The king was unhappy because no matter what he tried he could not make the monkeys behave. He tried force like his father had, it worked, but it also made them sneakier and he had to keep using it more and more. So he tried using bribery as had his uncle, to lure them in with their greed, and that worked too, but they became less responsible and were never satisfied or grateful. Then he'd tried making them see what was important was their own purpose and life meaning, but they became more shallow and only thought about their vain needs and cravings for attention and approval. But a bird had told him that there was a cave on Jade Mountain where lived a wise dragon. The Monkey King set out to find the dragon and ask him how to govern his people.

At the mouth of the cave the Monkey King found a green flute on the ground. Being curious he picked it up and blew. The most strange and haunting wail hung in the air. The king laughed, "Such a funny noise," and tossed the flute aside.

Presently the ground began to shake and the king could hear trees crashing and rocks quaking. When not from the cave but from out of the dense forest burst forth the Green Dragon. Its tail thrashed in the trees behind it. Its body coiled and uncoiled, muscular and slithering. Its head was haloed by mystical green fire, and from its mouth came smoke and flame.

'Who has summoned me!' demanded the dragon.

The Monkey King was very afraid as he spoke, 'I did.'

The Green Dragon's head expanded in flame, 'Who are you?' it boomed.

'I am the Monkey King,' said the Monkey King.

At this the dragon chuckled, 'Monkey

King?' it snorted, 'You are not the Monkey King," it hissed, laughing, "No one is king of the monkeys – they are impossible to rule. They do as they please and nothing pleases them for long. So called kings come and go. Fooling themselves – calling themselves their king. I ask again, who are you?'

The Monkey King took offence. 'Well, who are you?' demanded the Monkey King.

The dragon inhaled deeply and all the leaves and earth began to rise into the air as if weightless, until the Monkey King himself had to hold on to a nearby tree to keep from rising into the air. And then the dragon blew out his great breath and everything fell back to the ground and dented the earth where it fell as if heavier than it had ever been, including the Monkey King who felt as if he were now made of stone. 'I am that which arises and falls, sunrise and sunset, summer and winter, life and death. For that which has a season, I am that,' said the dragon. 'You have called me, so ask about what comes and passes away... Monkey King.'

The chastised Monkey King said then, 'You mean whatever influence I can make, whatever I try, passes away. You say the monkeys ultimately cannot be led.'

'I said, there is no way to rule them,' answered the Green Dragon, 'Neither force, nor greed, nor morality hold them. They are children who desire a father to look up to, but resent his authority.'

'Then they are doomed to chaos,' said the king.

'But...,' said the dragon, 'they can be led.'

'How?' asked the king.

'Monkeys are drawn to those who succeed. They will emulate the master, to get that for themselves,' said the dragon.

'Monkey see, monkey do?' the king said.

'Exactly,' said the Green Dragon, 'The question for you is," and it drew in its hot breath, 'What is success to a monkey?' "

And with that the master folded up his arms and looked over the fire at Dashi.

Dashi waited for there to be more. But when no more came, said at last, "That is not very encouraging master."

"Yes," said the master, "It is."

"But master, I don't know what monkeys, I mean, the people want," said Dashi.

"That doesn't matter," said the master, "What is important is that you always do what you think is important. To do this you need to be stubborn. Being stubborn, you have to not fall into the danger of being stuck. You must be able to free your mind to know it. It will tell you what is important to you. Then you can be freely stubborn, which will lead you to success. Then others will follow."

"You are saying that to lead is to sway people to see your kind of success as the success they are looking for," said Dashi.

The master said, "Those who's minds are free will freely desire your success as their own. They are your equals. Those who can be merely swayed think success is doing what the others think good. Their minds are not free to know for themselves what they desire. They are in some way stuck. They are also those who can just as easily be swayed away."

"So you need to keep them from other competing ideas," said Dashi.

"No," said the master firmly, "If you keep them from straying by isolating them from any other ideas what will happen is they will become more stuck and they will convert your great dream into a nightmare. It is why so many religions preach peace but their members act violently."

Dashi said, "So then how does one keep them? What is the most attractive kind of success?"

"Ah...Sacrificing your self for what you think other people want is thinking mind, not personal conviction. You must choose your path freely everyday, and with conviction act," said the master. "This is Jade Mountain," said the master knocking his knuckles on the green cave floor. Dashi saw, indeed it was. The whole cave was jade, all the way into the mountain's heart, and he wondered how he hadn't seen it.

"How do you choose your convictions, master?"

"If your minds are free they will find you," said the master, who chuckled. "They will find – you," and leaned forward pointing to Dashi's chest. The tea pot in the fire was now boiling, sending out random gusts of steam as the lid rattled ajar.

"Who I am," said Dashi.

The master lifted his eyebrows. "Indeed. Who are you?" said the master, a touch of steam playing about his smiling face, the flame reflected in this glistening eyes, opened wide.

This amused Dashi, "Master, the steam makes you look..."

The master stood and his cloak was turning green, "Who are you?" he insisted. His eyes became green fire, and he began to grow in size. "Who are you?!" he bellowed, green flame spreading all around, transforming by the second – as leaf and rock began to rise up, suspended in the air – into the Green Dragon. With deafening thunder the master's voice roared, "WHO ARE YOU?!"

Dashi awoke to the sound of the master's thunderous snoring. The master slumbered in his cot, one arm trailing out of the bed. Dashi was by the stove.

Lying in the dark, his heart's loud beating, reverberating echoes of the dream in his skull. Dashi bundled up all of who he thought he was, bore down on it in single minded focus, and burned it in a breath of fire.

In the ground Dashi made a long row for the mustard greens and placed seeds there.

"Master, explain why I shouldn't go and fight with the rebels, like my brother?" asked Dashi.

"Maybe you should," said the master, "Do you trust your mind in this?"

Dashi thought a moment, "No," he said, "I feel conflicted. I have meditated. I have tried to clear my mind."

"Do you think they need you? Do you think they will thank you? Do you think they will mourn you?" said the master, "If you truly thought you should be a highwayman as your brother, you would already be hiding in some forest with a dagger in your belt. You would never have been troubled enough to come to the mountain in the first place."

"I was troubled then, but now he has been killed, I feel cowardly not to go," said Dashi.

"Cowardice is felt only in comparison. I can also compare your wealth, or your physical prowess, or your intelligence. What is it to you that I compare? If you are moved to do something by the feelings you have for another, so be it. Great acts come from great hearts. But it is meaningless to do because of feeling that you should."

"Is that not a feeling too?" asked Dashi.

"Yes, a sticky one," said the master, "Note how when you try to take another perspective it doesn't let you go. It gnaws at you, it never leaves."

"Isn't acting out of love the same?" said Dashi.

"You mean the same love that possesses? That makes people prone to acts of madness? Love's a powerful addiction. There is no one view that is always right, not love, not compassion, not even trust. That is why one asks another for advise. Here is another mind where you are stuck." said the master.

"What I am feeling dogs me unceasingly. The feeling is unrelenting, and therefore I must seek to disengage from it. Is there something you suggest?" asked Dashi.

"Meditate. Burn away the impurities of your thoughts to make them simple. Also consider power. It is of value because everyone says so. If you have none then you are less significant than those that do. This is again comparison.

"A common flower in a field of flowers has little comparison value. But it may have meaning – to you. Comparison is measuring against what others think. Meaning is about what you see. Consider which drives your action."

Said Dashi, "But if I'm worried, not about myself, but about others or events, what then?"

"Escaping almost all worry," said the master, "requires trust. First in yourself – then because of that, in the good judgement of others. After, will come... a sense of the course of events."

"You do know the future then?" asked Dashi.

"Not know, only guess. But... ," said the master, "my guesses are very good."

Dashi said, "What is your guess, master?"

"The heavy taxes of the magistrate to pay for lavishments, inspires young men to become robbers. They harass the roads and cause disruption, both to survive and to try to bring attention to the curious going-ons at the palace of the magistrate. They steal food and give it to the people. A very odd thing for mere robbers to do. Their leaders are captured, accused of things they never did and tortured as examples.

"Every four years there is a new magistrate who arrives, but the policies remain identical. This is also odd. The situation worsens. Instead of suppressing the robbers, they make martyrs whose names are being whispered among the people.

The master smiled slyly, "Indeed formerly important persons have recently been seen with relatives of the martyrs. The people are emboldened. They tire of this state of affairs. The magistrate knows the people are displeased. Knows disruptions will increase.

"This will displease the provincial officials – and those higher up! – The magistrate will be found to be at fault! Something must be done immediately! Why?"

"To keep things as is," said Dashi.

"Quickly, Dashi – in what mind is the magistrate stuck?"

"Status," said Dashi.

Dashi walked up the path to the high meadow by himself. The master had given him a wide brimmed leather hat to wear and the condensing fog dripped off its brim. Dashi climbed higher into the clouds. Soon the mist was so thick that he walked in a haze and had to trust his feet to find their footing as he climbed. He carried the leather bag on his back for the roots the master had asked him to get. The weather was grey and cold and the master had decided, after a message arrived, that it was better that Dashi gather alone and that he should stay inside, where it was warm and create medicine packets.

The dark shapes of twisted tree trunks were but shadows and appeared in the distance as if people standing, watching. As the mists moved so did the shadows and Dashi watched them slowly dance in the dense clouds. The patter of dripping water from the trees created a slow and unpredictable rhythm that pulsed everywhere around him. Without the internal chatter, or that aimed at the master, as he walked, Dashi's minds were still. Dashi thought the master had wanted him to see this. He frequently paused, gazing at the shifting ghosts.

Over a small rise Dashi stopped. The light was brightening and he looked at the crowd of dark people before him, some seemed male and others female, some kindly held out their arms to him and others stood menacing. One stood distant to him, almost out of sight, up the next bank, but Dashi was sure it was the master looking down on him. "It would be just like him to sneak up here ahead of me, to make a point," though Dashi.

Dashi walked towards the tree and as he did, it looked more and more like the master standing there. Dashi could even make out the master's walking staff. "Master," Dashi called out," I see you," quickening his climbing pace. But as he neared the shadow, the mists began to part and he saw it was a tree with a broken branch leaning upon its trunk. Dashi passed this shadow by and went into the meadow out above the clouds.

The light was dazzling, clear and warm. The green meadow was now moving towards its ebb, as winter approached, but still the red berries, and drying seed pod heads nodded in the mountain air. All around the mountain an ocean of white clouds, all the way to the horizon, with a dome of pure blue above it.

Dashi took out his knife for hunting the root, and put down the pack but continued staring at the world above the clouds. A horizon of white met his eye in all directions, only punctuated by distant mountain peaks. It looked like snowy rolling hills.

"Thank you master," he said aloud. Dashi thought, "He wanted me to experience this too. The shadows, the parting of the clouds, and to come to sight that was clear, and far. And then, to gather medicine, because it is good to also be practical." Dashi looked up at the sky, "On my own." Dashi smiled and set about filling the bag.

After, Dashi took out the small lunch he'd brought and ate it, he lay back cloud gazing almost not wanting to leave this perfect moment. But the roots were needed by someone, and so with pack over his back he began his descent back into the mist and shadow. He marched down the lonely path. As he went he could feel the weight of the pack, the fall of his shoe by root and rock, the rain pattering on his hat, the smell of the forest and how it changed, including the smell of smoke that he thought must be rising up from the town below, as people stoked their fires against the chill. It was raining now.

But as Dashi came closer and closer to the shack the smell of smoke became more acrid and now beneath the clouds he could see a large plume rising into the air. Dashi ran. Even through the rain, over tangled root and rock and rain he ran, his breath steaming behind him like he was on fire. Until at last he came to the roof blackened shack, hissing smoke rolling up into the sky.

Dashi saw the hoof prints and boot prints in the wet earth. "Master!" cried Dashi, and scrambled forward through the mud. He burst inside the shack. But the master was gone.

The shack had mostly survived. The rain had saved it. Only the thatch in one corner had burned through, the far wall underneath the hole smeared with sooty weeping water.

Dashi stood in the corner. Rain pelting him. A numbness froze in his limbs and will.

Suddenly anger gripped him. Dashi ran outside, and climbed up to the roof and threw off the smouldering thatch and began patching it with thatch stolen from the rest of the roof. Much was blackened but not burned.

His face, hands, arms, chest and legs were soot black. But he worked instead of despairing. His eyes stung. But he mended instead of dissolving into recrimination.

It was only when the roof was once again whole that he went inside, and saw the master's staff leaning by his bed, that he remembered the vision in the mist.

Three days later Dashi went down to the town, but instead of entering the gates he wandered among the shacks littered outside its walls, being careful not be be seen by the guards. The mud sucked at his shoes as he slunk through the narrow walkways.

"Dashi," said an old woman standing outside her dwelling of mud and straw.

"Nanno, how are you?" asked Dashi.

"Do you have food in your pack?" Nanno asked.

"I do, and some medicine," said Dashi.

"Then I am well," she replied, "Come into my home," she said and beckoned Dashi into her tiny shelter. Dashi removed his shoes and ducked his head under the low door. "Bring them in, or someone will take them," she said.

Dashi sat at the low table and she made them cups of hot water. "Those who have taken to the road are scattered. Since your brother was captured they have not been able to find their courage. Now are you returning to take your brother's place?"

"No," said Dashi.

"Then why are you here at all?" she asked.

"I wish to know what is happening. What news is there?" he said.

She narrowed her eyes at Dashi, "News? We work in the fields, but cannot live close-by because the magistrate forbids it. We live here, in this sty. We are hungry. But we cannot hunt because the magistrate forbids it. Your brother, at least, gave us food."

Dashi fished some edible roots he had gathered out of his pack and put them on the table, along with a packet of fresh medicines the master had previously given for the cold months. "And died in jail," defended Dashi, "I bring food. Not much, but there isn't much."

Nanno grabbed up the food to her chest as though he might snatch it back, "He died a hero, which is more than I can say for you. At least there is forage on your mountain What have we here?" she said, "Your master got to live on the mountain and we have to huddle here starving. Why is that? - Birds and flowers," she said nodding slowly. "Birds and flowers."

"I don't know what you mean by that," said Dashi.

"Ha!" she exclaimed, "You don't either... do you? Always thought your brother was the smart one. You've had your head in the clouds from the moment you were born. Go back over there, far away, Dashi. If you won't be a real man and fight, we don't need whatever you or your dead master is pedalling."

Dashi's eyes flared anger, "Wisdom," scolded Dashi, "More wisdom that you'll ever have, Nanno... and one day I will bring down the magistrate for what he has done to my master."

The old woman looked shocked, and then

burst into howls of laughter, "Hee!?" she laughed, "Hee, he!?" she shrieked, "O my, O... what a fool you are."

Dashi left her hut and because he was mad stepped outside into the mud and then had to reach back inside for his shoes, only causing the old woman to renew her derisive laughter. The people stood around watching. Dashi left in a huff and they, not even knowing why they should, jeered.

Winter came. Dashi remained on the mountain. He and the master had already put up enough supplies, and fortunately most of them had not been affected by the fire. Those that were, Dashi ate first.

He meditated every day on the fire within, as the master had taught. He consumed the fire so that it did not consume him. But when he wasn't meditating, he had a lot of time to think. Making fuel for the fire.

All the different hurts mixed together until they started to join, seeking some simple answer. Grieving deeply and remembering gratitude, breathing out and breathing in. Sometimes they would merge. Grateful for his grief, of having even known the master he'd lost. Dashi however didn't grieve his gratitude as he felt that more 'sticky,' like pushing a wagon backwards. Moreover he saw life was both sweet and sour – each creating the conditions for the other.

While underneath, the question from the dragon remained, "Who are you?"

"Who is the you that asks who I am?"

"For that matter – who is the dragon?"

"Who is the magistrate?"

"Who," he thought, "was my brother?"

Nanno told him; his brother was a hero – the myth well under way. Yes, he ordered his men to bring the people food, but Dashi knew it was only when they captured too much for the band to eat before it spoiled. But this hero got captured, and died, and never freed anyone.

While true, the magistrate was the villain, every hero needs a tyrant to exist. There is no act filled with more pride than that of the false martyr. His brother relished his position, being a bandit, being admired.

It was that more than anything that had sent Dashi up the mountain in search of a more honourable way of life. Nanno, and the others thought him a coward because he refused to throw himself at the magistrate's walls. Being approved of by others, and making that your goal are two completely different things. People who imagine themselves heroes and martyrs think they know who they are: but they only follow a map and never look up – until it's too late.

Still Dashi's pride felt the accusation's sting, and the arising righteous anger made him desire to punish the fools.

"Just like the master had said, it's agreement I want. How like the magistrate I am, then," thought Dashi, "The master knew it very well, right from the beginning and tried to get me to see it too."

"Who was the master?"

"The master..." began Dashi, his thought changing.

"What a poor student I was," he thought. "I should have learned more when he was here. No, not should, the master had said, but to be in the right mind to want to."

Dashi thought, "And now am I the vessel of his teachings?"

"Who are you?"

"What does that even mean? I'm only slowly understanding.

"What is a who? ... a preference for mind? My brother, the magistrate, myself – they all have their mind preferences. Even my master.

"Just like the master said. To know the mind they use, that I have also, is to know their values. By knowing that mind within me, allows me to understand as they do. And if they are stuck, then to know oneself in stuckness. That is how we understand each other – from the inside out.

"That which is within, the minds, to the degree we are aware – we understand who. Both them and us. To be unstuck, to be able to enter into all minds is to enter the mind of the other and find they are not other, but yourself.

"Easy with those who agree. Begin there. The other requires the mind that you would not see in yourself. Opening the door to everyone's mind, there is no enemy, except the one you chose not to understand – the mirror of what you refuse of yourself."

"This is why it was so hard for the master to explain this simply," thought Dashi. "How do you speak to the mind that will not listen?"

"Who are you?"

"There is no simple answer, no definitive answer, because as you move about in your minds the answer is changing. But, I am: all that and whatever it opens onto. I am:

the peculiar condition of my natural preference. And rejection does not change who I am; it doesn't even hide it, it amplifies it. Any eyes that can see, see it's only myself who's fooled - thinking I've cut away my shadow and unaware how long behind me it grows."

Dashi breathed in and brought his breath down to bear upon, "Who is Dashi?" Grateful that he could begin to leave behind the humiliating self deception.

Over the winter, he found laughter's mind when he thought too much, or tried to second guess himself, how he should be. And smiled when one day he saw nothing was against him. It was just the world, as it had always been.

Slowly a peace came to Dashi. He grew a sense of humour. His mind became as quicksilver, his heart as glowing fire. And spring came to the mountain.

One day Dashi realised the shack was a mess. He'd not bothered tidying or cleaning in some weeks, and this he began to set straight. He had not ever bothered to put away the roots he had collected on the day he'd come back to find the master taken away. He had been stumbling across it and ignoring it. He wondered if they'd become mouldy in the bag, but upon opening saw they had only dried. Dashi began to load the roots into the large box where the master kept his herbs. It was quite empty and was therefore easy to fit the medicinal roots inside. Its emptiness mirrored his mood.

"Self pity is the worst poison. Every little indignity festers," he thought, and set to shift to a happier mind. "For this, happiness is the antidote."

"Why is the box empty?" asked a mind.

Dashi blinked.

He now removed the roots from the box and placed them back into the bag which he slung across his shoulder, taking the staff, he left the cabin, winding his way down through the forest, and through the muddy roads and shacks to the town where he approached the gate, showing the guards the roots he carried, giving them a false name, then making his way along the back alleys past the herbalist, finally to the home of the older woman, and there knocked on the door, which was opened by the young woman whose face showed no expression of surprise in seeing him, and she let him into the gloom where the older woman was no longer in her bed, and she closed the door behind him.

Dashi said aloud, "Master, I have brought your staff."

"About time," said the master from the kitchen.

"We are both dead," said the master seated at the table in the steamy kitchen.

"Funny, I felt all right this morning," laughed Dashi.

"Indeed," said the master, "I thought it was just a cough. However officially we are both dead, as ordered by... I suspect someone in the magistrate's house."

"The former jailor?" asked Dashi.

"No," said the master.

"Your wife?" asked Dashi.

The master smiled and nodded.

Dashi asked, "What became of her sister?"

"I had her moved to somewhere safer," said the master and Dashi felt in the master a deeper current of strategic intention.

Dashi trusted this sense. "She is influential," said Dashi.

"She is known by those who are exceedingly powerful, and she was favoured. - More so than her sister," said the master smiling.

"She lived at court," said Dashi.

"Yes."

"As did you," said Dashi.

"Yes," said the master.

"Did you love her?"

"I still do," said the master. "However, I was made to marry her younger sister."

"Who was not at court," said Dashi.

"Oh, she was. But only by her older sister's graces. But my wife had designs on a prize that another woman with more power sought. This was all our undoing.

"Knowing of my love for her older sister, it was arranged that I should marry the younger. This squelched my wife's designs and also punished my love for allowing her younger sister into the court.

"Not long after that, I was given a new position. I was sent far away. A northern posting, where one was normally sent as a sentence, in shame. I was made magistrate in a little town, under a mountain. It was supposed to only be for four years, but strangely my name continued to be chosen, at random.

"My wife's older sister finally left court and chose banishment, near me, rather than stay where she had everything. But paradoxically in renouncing our worldly power, positions and responsibilities we found peace."

"You were magistrate," said Dashi.

"I was," replied the master.

"You said your wife married a wealthy man after you," said Dashi.

The master smiled and raised his eyebrows, "She married the magistrate who replaced me," said the master, "But he died years ago."

"So who replaced him?" asked Dashi.

"No one," said the master.

"But who..."

"My former wife," said the master, "It is she who impersonates the magistrate. Whispers about the town have been this for years. You never gossiped in the right kind of circles, Dashi."

"Master," said Dashi, "She has been causing much hardship. Do you not think it your responsibility to reclaim your power – for the good of the people?"

The master said, "Dashi, you have come so far and yet you persist in this. Let me explain. When the magistrate who replaced me, and married my wife, died, my wife and the jailor colluded. Anyone who knew of the magistrate's death was arrested and killed. Or those who were too well protected but amenable to bribe, became collaborators.

"My wife's new friends require lavish living for their complicity, so taxes rise. She flatters them with meaningless titles, and elite offices in which they do nothing and are never involved. The least of their children are palace guards, who stand about with spears, but do not know the sharp end from the dull.

"Together they succeeded in hiding their swindle from the provincial officials. As far as any there is concerned, and no one is, the magistrates of this unimportant and cursed post are alive and well.

"But..." said Dashi.

"And should ever anyone need an audience with the magistrate, they will see the jailor in disguise. Mostly audiences will meet the magistrate's wife, who relays his wishes... With apologies of course."

"Of course," said Dashi.

"But it is she who rules. Who is to question this state of affairs? Apparently that is the calibre of magistrate sent here. They all go a bit mad, like he of the birds and flowers, who went mad and resigned his station, preferring to wander off into the fields.

"Birds and flowers," Dashi said to himself remembering.

"This is what I am called. Otherwise, every single one since has met some tragic death near the end of his term. All part of the curse of the mountain. In truth, once the glorious pageantry of their installation is over, they are gutted like a goose in the dungeon, and we have four more years of..."

"Attacking us," said Dashi.

"Blaming you," said the master, "The last two magistrates were killed by the godless robbers who live in the forest. I explain this so that you can see what claiming this power actually means. Going into the snake's nest to remove them."

"But surely deceitfulness cannot be allowed to continue," implored Dashi.

The master looked off as if looking a far distance. He picked up his tea and then set it back down without drinking. "To answer your question," said the master, "No. It is not my responsibility, nor duty. Like you, I have much compassion, but little power. I gave it up because the weight of it calls you to decide, for the people, what should weigh upon them. No one person should be asked to bear life and death. The people, of your great concern, shirk their duty and call it someone else's. This, the first deception, that of the self, allows for anything done thereafter."

"So then I should take on my responsibility and fight," said Dashi.

"If you have power, or feel impelled that throwing your life into the fire will achieve something. Go right ahead. But shift your mind to see whether this is really just someone else's story? Is this meaningful to you? It isn't just this insisting mind, trust must allow all to answer, and then you judge."

"I do understand master," said Dashi, "It has to come from the right place. But still I worry about the people."

Said the master, "You will be driven mad wishing to change things you do not have the power to change. You cannot move the people from their lie, because it serves them. When conditions are so terrible the people become ready for change, then act. For now, use the one power you do have - change to another mind, and then let's continue."

"Yes, master," said Dashi, recentring himself. He took his feeling of concern and allowed it to leave and soon what replaced it was another sense. A sense of humour. He trusted the new mind to speak.

"Master, I think to stop people in their constant infighting and awaken them to kindness would take heaven falling to earth."

"Indeed," laughed the master, "To be grateful and content, to have a full belly, and loved ones, and a roof over your head and to work a craft as holy offering. You would think this was enough."

The master leaned back, "When I was magistrate I thought it best to be tolerant and kind. I thought this would serve as an example to the people. So I never punished harshly, and the thieves came out of the gutters like rats.

"The people suffered under my tolerance, and hated me for it. I thought it was me they hated. That I was as good as having nobody because I could not bring myself to be cruel even to such thieves. The people wanted a ruler. So I left. In fifteen years with the full power of magistrate I was unable to affect change.

"The provincial officials were furious. They sent a harsh man, with a harsh rule to deal with the people. He got rid of the thieves, but the people hated him too. They petitioned to have him removed. This was ignored. For the province, this is not an important area, and they do not care that it is ruled brutally.

"After his death the province sent a new magistrate. Who... I've explained. But it wouldn't matter if the people knew about my wife's cabal of friends. My former wife has merely exemplified an unpopular but highly successful style of rule. The people don't like anything, nor nothing. I realise now, what does not address the root of their grief is meaningless."

"Which is..." said Dashi.

"Which is, they insist on being absolutely free – free of responsibility. So much so, the people feel free to hate, because they bear no responsibility for that hatred. And because it makes them easier to rule, the rulers tacitly condone that they stay as children. Thus enemies of the state arise whenever it suits, and the people bark like mad dogs at the moon.

"It doesn't matter the ruler. It is their own false god of freedom from which their minds need freeing."

Dashi shook his head, "Still the provincial officials would not be pleased to know they had been deceived."

"Ahh...," said the master, "Yes. She has a secret. She has borrowed power, but never really understood its nature, except that it meant she could do to others what they could not do to her. That is why she is so dangerous.

"Her sister and I she suspects of merely biding our time, because she does not understand we do not want her power. She mistakes our kindness for cunning, and our open presence as indication of a challenge, of mutual destruction. I have sent messages through her sister, but these have fallen on deaf ears."

"She thinks you have a plan," said Dashi.

"She knows we are resourceful," said the master.

"It's why you sent her sister away," stated Dashi.

"Partially," said the master.

"But she sent guards to arrest you," said Dashi.

"To kill me," said the master, "And you, I'm afraid. Apparently she is desperate enough to call what she sees as our bluff. I sent you up onto the mountain because of the letter. The guards had been ordered that day up onto the mountain. I slipped away..."

"With your medicines," said Dashi.

The master nodded, "They wouldn't have noticed," said the master, "I stashed them and then hid to watch if they would come."

"She must be frantic to find us, and stop us," said Dashi.

The master said, "And yet you entered the city without incident. I have noticed no guard running about, no increased movements."

Dashi thought. "The guards lied."

"They were afraid to say we'd slipped their grasp. Wouldn't you be?" asked the master.

"So now we are dead," said Dashi, nodding, "You are right master. What would being a hero get me?"

"Too intellectual. And, I am not right – you are justifying. It is simple. Look inside. If you are stuck, get unstuck. After awhile it becomes easy. You just do what is there," said the master, "Maybe you will run into the burning building to save someone. Maybe you will feel sad because of their terrible fate. Should do, is from other people. Freely feel what is from you."

"What I feel is that we should return to the cabin," said Dashi, "I fixed the roof, it wasn't too badly damaged. We can go any time."

"I think," said the master, "when this is over I will either be really dead, or I will be back in my place as magistrate."

"I thought you just said..."

"You can have the cabin, Dashi. I will come visit you when I can," said the master.

"If you live, you mean," said Dashi.

"In any case," said the master.

The master spoke quietly to the young woman in the main room while Dashi ate his breakfast. "Yes, grandfather," Dashi thought he heard her say.

She left and not much later returned and spoke to the master.

"Your timing is excellent, Dashi," said the master, "The plan is already in motion. You will get to see the show."

"Will there be puppets?" joked Dashi.

"Many," replied the master.

Later in the night, Dashi was awakened by the sound of someone briefly rapping on the outside wall. Then, came a short reply, from inside. Rising, Dashi could see a candle was lit in the kitchen and found the young woman there.

Groggy, Dashi said, "An odd time of the night for mysterious noises."

To which she replied, "What better time for odd noises?"

"You *are* his granddaughter," said Dashi.

It was odd. Dashi watched the master change out of his simple robe and into the robe of a magistrate. It was a little large for him now.

"I was more full of myself then," the master joked, "The fancy robes aren't just for show: they masquerade the lie. Better to let someone else make the hard decisions that governance requires." The master stood tall. "Perhaps this is why I do not feel so offended by a false magistrate. In some sense it is more truthful."

Even as one who left his office he was impressive. Dashi felt conflicted. He was attracted to the power, but repelled by its use. "Master, do you want to return to being magistrate?" he asked.

The master laughed, "Heavens no," he said, "But I don't like being hunted either." He adjusted his robes. "Most animals prefer to be left in peace, but if you poke at them long enough, and if they do not wish to run, they will come at you, all teeth and claws. How do I look?"

"You look very official," said Dashi.

"I look like a fool," said the master, "and not the right kind either. Time to go, Dashi."

"Where are we headed?" he asked getting the master's staff. It had been several days since Dashi had arrived and they'd stayed inside hiding the whole time.

The master took it from Dashi, "We? *I* am going to meet a friend of a friend."

The master covered his magistrate's robe under sack cloth. He was about to leave when Dashi blocked the door, "Master, I am coming with you."

"You are returning to the mountain, remember?" said the master.

"But master you just told me that one should not involve oneself," said Dashi.

"I told you, you must free your mind, and only then can you freely decide. If force of arms rules the day then I freely accept that I will likely die. My plan is not to. But I do not wish to lose my love. I do not wish to be hunted. I do not wish to lose my home. My ex-wife has put this all in danger. So I will freely run into the burning building."

"I too will likely be hunted," said Dashi, "That is what they do to godless robbers. I trust my trust, and I trust you. If this is your path, then that is the only path I trust." He stood resolute, blocking the door.

The master's eyes became teary, "I consider you as a son. A parent ultimately cannot protect a child from the world. I did not say, but I once had a son - not by my wife - who died... mysteriously."

"I have suspected this," sighed Dashi.

"I could not face the truth then, so I rejected my position. I am sorry this failing of mine has caused so much grief. And maybe your death. But I am glad you will be with me," said the master putting his hand on Dashi's shoulder. "Come, we need take our tactical position."

"What a little food can do," said the master.

The square in front of the magistrate's palace was full of protesting people. Because the square was also full of guards standing at the gate, the master and Dashi stood in the shadows, watching.

"Today your people are feasting and it is the towns people who go hungry," said the master.

"You did that?" asked Dashi.

"No, you did."

Dashi blinked, "Sorry, master, did you say...?"

"Yes, you gave the order, via the network or course. Your men received the plan and have carried out your orders. It was fabulously successful - the tactics, the strategy - brilliant! They know now that you were just biding your time after the death of your brother - to make the guard think they had succeeded, and therefore to stop pursuing your men. By staying out of sight, pretending you were dead, you protected them. They have deep respect for you, Dashi."

"That's not what..."

"A true leader doesn't have to explain," said the master, holding up his hand. "Now, regard the weapons."

Dashi noted the new rifles the guards carried. He wondered whether they knew how to use them.

"Is this where we are meeting your friend?" asked Dashi.

"We are waiting for him to come. Then we will go together," said the master.

"Where?" asked Dashi.

The master smiled, "Why, into the jaws of the dragon."

"What about all the guards, master?" asked Dashi.

A hand clamped on both of their shoulders, "Yes, master, what about the guards?" Dashi turned and saw the captain of the guards. And that some of the people who had been milling about, now closing in on them were guards in disguise. "I remember you two," he said to his men. "Look, we've caught the drunken pack horse and his master again."

The captain squinted suspiciously at the master's clothes, and seeing a hint of the robe beneath, grabbed his collar and tore his sack cloth disguise. "And where did you come to acquire such fine clothes mule master?" he said jeering, "Thieves meet a thieves end – on a rope."

"They are my own. I am the magistrate of birds and flowers," the master said switching into the diction of the court, "Look into my eyes and trust what you feel." The master stared into the eyes of the captain.

The captain did not look happy. It was now evident on his face that he'd caught a whale and not a minnow, and didn't know what to do.

The master said very quietly, "Very soon, an official from the provincial ruler will be arriving with my ex-wife's sister. She, as a favoured person of the emperor's father has requested this, and he of course has acquiesced. He is an old acquaintance of ours and also of the current magistrate. He will know him by sight."

The captain licked his lips nervously.

The master continued, "All you need do is await their arrival for confirmation of what I have said. Should I be lying then you and your men can slip away quietly with us and do what you reported you did when your men set my shack on fire. Another sad ending for a retired magistrate."

The captain swallowed.

The master said, "However, should I be telling the truth... You are no fool captain. I know what you know. They will request to see the magistrate. To keep up appearances the order will come to let them in. What then?"

The captain blinked.

The master whispered, "The whole entourage can't be murdered by... highway robbers. The official coming is too important. There will be an investigation. Should I, the former magistrate and my student disappear rather than meeting with them, then again there will be an investigation." The master leaned even closer, "It is a very large entourage. Your first responsibility, captain, is to your men."

At that the captain's eyes went wide. He bowed slowly, almost imperceptibly.

"Well, don't be causing any trouble," he said, releasing them and slapped Dashi on the back of the head. Saying nothing else, but with gestures to his men he drew them back to the periphery.

Dashi rubbed his head. "Ow. Of all the bad luck..."

"Bad luck? That was no bad luck. That was my plan," said the master, "I mean, your plan. I saw them as soon as we arrived. The captain and his guards are too big and well fed, they can't hide amongst the rabble. Even the townsfolk are looking a bit thin."

"Master..." began Dashi.

"Hush," said the master, "Save your questions. Just watch."

Dashi watched the square. The people ranted, no longer able to contain themselves, they swore at the stoney faced guards. Dashi watched the people. He breathed in their desperation. But he also remembered the words of his master, standing sentinel, calmly awaiting delivery or death. "Were the people ready now?" thought Dashi. Surely in times of extremity even the comfortable lie may be put to rest.

At one point Dashi saw the captain of the guards go in through the gate. The people made as if to rush forward, but edged back under the aim of rifles and point of bayonet. Only a few minutes later he exited, with the same effect, the swelling crowd's wave breaking against the guard's shore. The captain left the square with his men.

Some time later the sound of bells, and horse and carriage could be heard, then the faint music, then the footfalls. Soon the procession came into the square: eight bearers marching with colourful banners, several swinging smoking censers, behind, those carrying ceremonial carved wooden boxes as long as your arm, and gentlemen attendants, and after all this, the large intricately carved and gold inlayed carriage.

"That is a very ample carriage for just two people," commented the master.

The captain and his men rode their horses beside the carriage, pushing the crowd back. The crowd parted in front of the horse's hooves but shouted all at once, a cacophony of sorrows: no food! we are staving! remove the tyrant! someone better fix this! The captain drew out a whistle from sage to the dungeon wide. The sticky colognes of cave and iron, sweat and urine, body and sick, haunted like incense.

The master and he quickly hid, crouched down behind a bale of wet mildewing straw. Roughly oval, the cells lined the walls, and in its centre a large area with heavy wooden tables, bound with iron, and with chains and manacles, and straps. Cast on the floor underfoot, the straw was a dark maroon stain.

On the two great tables, wide leather straps held down a man and woman, bound to their surfaces face down. Both of their clothing had been ripped away, exposing their bleeding backs, as now the lash came down from the hand of a brutish-built man, in a black hood. "The official and the sister have been captured!" thought Dashi.

Dashi could not help but wonder, if this was the way his brother was murdered. His head was ringing. He watched, transfixed, by the flayed blood, glistening red, flying up to dot the dark brown ceiling as the torturer pulled back his stroke to flog them yet again. Dashi missed that the master had already skirted around the room. Yes, they would rush the torturer together and put an end to this.

inside his coat and blew it.

At once the gates began to open. Inside Dashi could see more nervous guards armed with spears.

"Come on," said the master grabbing Dashi's arm, dragging him quickly through the shouting crowd. The procession passed through and then the carriage and the guards inside were hurryingly closing the gate again. The master pushing through the edge of the crowd stepped through the gates pulling Dashi behind him. All at once spears were levelled at them. The crowd drew back.

The clip clop of hooves came behind them. Dashi looked back at the captain. The captain nodded to the guard. "The magistrate of birds and flowers returns to see his fellow magistrate," said the captain, and turned his horse to face the crowd. At that the spears were put up. And the gate began to close again.

Dashi kept looking at the captain's back as the gates were closing. What mind was this? Honour? Self preservation? We were nothing, indeed a loose end to be tied up, then we were a potentially threat, but he let us go. How did he know the story the master told was true? True enough to put himself at risk? He didn't know us. "It isn't us he trusts," said Dashi, realising "It's his own judgement."

The gates closed.

"I told him the truth," said the master, "But only someone of courage is willing to hear it." The master took Dashi's arm. "Our captain is a betting man, and therefore prides himself as something of a strategist. He was not born noble, and has therefore risen on his wits."

The carriage was already far ahead, the master pulled young Dashi after him. "I suggest we do the same." And the two broke into a run.

Dashi and the master ran the long distance through the inner gates, finding the carriage, sitting alone, and empty, where it had stopped beneath the grand stairway to the great hall's doors, that stood gaping open.

The master boosted himself up to look into the carriage. "As I suspected, boxes."

The two hurried up the steps. "Boxes?" thought Dashi. The master moved more slowly as they approached the doors. Inside

Dashi could see the great pillars, the long intricately tiled floor, the far stairs rising up to the great seat of the magistrate.

Dashi and the master entered, but the hall was empty. A couple spears lay abandoned on the floor.

"There should be a guard at each," said the master point to the green banner draped pillars, "Good." The master looked towards the top of the stairs. He grew very quiet, and his smile faded. He motioned for Dashi to be silent and pointed. Dashi saw it now, a body, motionless, its pool of blood spreading out to drip down the stairs.

The master led Dashi quietly up the stairs past the great chair and the body of the unknown man and in through a secret door that opened to a long unlit hallway. On either side of the hallway from the ceiling to half way to the floor it was lined with horizontal blinds as partitions, behind which were small rooms. These lighted slits striped the dim walls. From here in the dark of the hallway one could see into every room. In this secret place there were no secrets possible.

The master indicated they crouch low as they went so as not to be seen. Dashi stepped in something wet, and was glad for the dim light. They came to an intersecting hall. The master turned them left, then stopped, as if remembering. He went right. They slowly crept, half bent over.

The walls became ever more decorated. From somewhere far within the palace, echoing up the passage, there were cries of pain, and incomprehensible shouting. The rooms seemed to go on and on. They would stop at large doors, quickly passing them, or running stealthily into great empty rooms and then quietly, always into side corridors. The fighting that was clearly happening, the sound of metal hitting metal, the tumult of shouting, was drawing closer.

Down a narrow twisting course they wound. Until the master stopped at a wall and feeling in the wall a crack, he slid open a hidden door. Looking over his shoulder at Dashi, he put his fingers to his lips. And they entered the dark way.

The master indicated for Dashi to put his one hand on the wall and the other on the master's shoulder. Dashi put his hand on the wall. It was cold stone. The master slid the door back into place and they were enveloped in primal darkness.

At once the master began to inch his way forward. Dashi followed, picking his feet up lest there be anything to trip on. The master would abruptly change directions around a corner. Dashi had to concentrate least he be spun off to stumble away into the dark. But always he could hear the master's left hand slapping upon the wall.

In the disorienting void Dashi's hearing inflamed. He heard his own breathing, his lips parting, his swallowing. In the dark, the loud echoing of sobbing and moaning, penetrated from all directions. The sounds of an inescapable hell pit as something in the black scurried away from his feet. He heard the screams of pain coming closer, the preceding smack of something hard.

Presently a crack of light appeared. Slowly they moved towards the crack and Dashi could see the outline of the master putting his eye to it. The sobs and blows came from this room beyond the hidden passage. And the whisper of a terrible stench.

"This is the truth," said the master, "See it. But remain calm."

Dashi braced himself for whatever would be next. The master put his fingers in the crack in the secret door and slid the pas-

He was surprised to see then, the master walking slowly out into the middle of the room. Dashi looked over the top of the bale, watching him talk with a plumpish man, dressed in royal blue, and a woman in embroidered lavender, as if not a few steps away there was not bloody brutality. Dashi realised, what he hadn't seen. All around the walls, stationed in the shadows between every cell was another black hooded man.

The master waved Dashi to join them. Dashi feigned his carriage over to them and bowed, his face as calm as he could make it. What is happening? Dashi recognised the woman as from on the bed in the dim room, his master's lover. It was not she on the torture table.

"This is my student," said the master to the fleshy man in blue silk to whom he'd been speaking.

"Your honoured master has made me understand the situation. I extend my condolences for your brother's death. For what it is worth, I shall see a citation is issued to your brother, for his heroism, and of course a general pardon for your band of fighters – fighting against this outrageous usurpation of imperial power."

Dashi glanced at the master, he breathed

in, "I don't know what to say," said Dashi, "Thank you."

The blue man raised a pudgy fingered hand to his unusually red lips, "It is we who have not been paying proper attention to this situation, to our chagrin and shame. But that which our lady has made evident to us we will now put right. The provincial governor has made it expressly clear to me that this matter should be... resolved. We were just discussing the matter of appointing a new magistrate," he said.

"Sadly, I am already dead," said the master.

"Yes," said the blue man, annoyed, "I am trying to engage your master to once again take up the position, but he bends like a young tree in the wind and I cannot grasp him."

"What about," the sister spoke up from her silence, "if Dashi should be the new magistrate?" Both the master and the blue man turned to look at her. "True he has no hold in court but out on the edge of the empire that may be to his advantage. These are his people. The fighters followed his brother. And since his execution, it is Dashi who is the natural heir. I have observed him and see he follows his own line of mind."

"He is truly relentless," confirmed the master.

"Also," continued the sister, casting her eye on Dashi's master, "My granddaughter is a sharp judge of character and says that he is honourable, and truthful, and courageous of spirit."

The master nodded sighing, "He has always shown a stubborn streak of concern for the state of the people. I have tried to rub it out, but alas have been unable to." He turned to look at Dashi as though regarding the purchase of a horse. "Although I deem it akin to punishment, it would perhaps be best for his continued education that he be allowed to become magistrate. I give my assent... should he choose it."

"A glorious position for one so young," said the blue man, "Even without education, you could still go far."

The master looked Dashi right in the eyes, "With this power you could make whatever changes you desire. However, even out here, you are ultimately an agent of the state. The empire will outlive us both, and beyond its dissolution will be another, and another." The master emphasised each word, "Do you understand?"

"But power can be used for the good,"

said Dashi.

"There you go," said the master one palm held up, "He is unfathomably idealistic."

"It isn't such a bad thing," said the older sister, "I recall you having this vein yourself," she said. The older sister glanced in the direction of her moaning younger sister. "There comes a time when sentiment runs out. When tolerance can no longer be tolerated. Dashi has not come to this. Let the young be young," she said.

"I bow to your wisdom," said the master, and then he did. The master removed his robe and placed in over Dashi's shoulders.

The blue man slapped his fleshy palms together with a sound like a bucket of dough upended onto the floor, "Splendid. Dashi, I hereby appoint you as the new magistrate. I have taken the liberty to begin the dispensing of justice. However as I am now in your jurisdiction, what shall we do with these two?"

Dashi felt shocked, frozen, horrified, stuck. Here was the power to change things. Dashi knew why the people shrank from it. This kind of power was no life giving light, it was no prize, it was and had always been a flame used to scour the darkness

Dashi looked around at the younger sister and the man he assumed was the jailor. They had killed his brother. They had killed countless others. They had tried to kill him and his master, and probably her own sister had the master not sent her to fetch the blue man.

But hate was for the powerless. He allowed those feelings to fall away. Instead he felt pity for the fate they had made for themselves. Even when they had duped everyone, had stolen everything, they could not be content. They had to continue even when they should take their pillage and retreat. Dashi knew they lived in worry, bathed in worry, dreamed of worry.

Being stuck in their fear of downfall, had led to their downfall.

The master had warned him, but this lesson he needed to see for himself. Centring, he sighed, as he came to a calm space. He understood. The unconditional trust of one's minds, even if fallible, it was the freedom from all worrying. "What about the people, Dashi?" said one of his minds sarcastically, "Free their minds," came the answer from another. Dashi looked at the two.

What should happen? Dashi no longer believed in shoulds.

What was the prescribed goal? There was no goal, only centring and clarity of mind.

"I feel," began Dashi, "Their wounding of the people, this town – I will have to bind and heal. I am moved by their suffering, but their madness has gone too far to be helped. If they are beyond my master's help, then they are beyond my ability to help.

"Impersonating a magistrate is a crime above that of a magistrate to assess. It should be dealt with, certainly at the level of the provincial capitol, if not the imperial capitol. However, I have been led to understand there is a woman at the imperial capitol who would take too much pleasure in their demise. I do not wish for her to deepen her own distemper any further than she has done on her own. And for my master and his lady I think this return would taint even this dark ending. So, I am transferring them to the jurisdiction of the provincial capitol. I do not wish them any more pain, but it will be for the judges there to find compassion," he said, "I wish it were different."

Dashi addressed the torturer, his torturer, "No more."

Dashi looked at the blue man, "I assume you are leaving for the capitol after a rest here. If we provide a means of transport would your entourage accompany the prisoners?"

The blue man wiped away a tear, and grew a big smile. "As you wish, I, will deliver the prisoners back to the capitol to face justice," he said sighing. The plump blue official put his arm out for the sister to take and they left the dungeon together, "Well chosen madame."

Dashi heard her say, "He deliberates like a sage."

The master put a comforting hand on Dashi's back as they followed. "You have already made a much better decision than I ever would have. I could never do it. But then I didn't have such a wise master."

"Master," said Dashi, following them, "I have just calmly sent two people to their likely deaths. How shall I face myself?"

"Doing what you feel is right, does not make it easy. That is why the people hide from it, and the courageous temper their characters into scythes," said the master, "My ex-wife will however get her day of fame. Perhaps you understand her better than you think."

"It is sad, master," said Dashi.

"It is sad," agreed the master as they ascended the stairs, "It is a regrettable necessity: those who would use power... when the people don't want it. It is an enslaving state of mind to seek power over others, just as it is an unnatural state to forever tolerate power over yourself – that is what I have learned."

Dashi looked at the master.

"You think I don't still learn things?" said the master, "I've learned so much from you, I could write a book."

They had returned to the corridors of the palace – Dashi's palace. Dashi gazed around him, silent, wondering what he had gotten himself into and looked imploringly at his master.

The master laughed, "In fact, I consider you one of my greatest teachers." He bowed, "Thank you, master," said the master.

www.ingramcontent.com/pod-product-compliance
Lightning Source LLC
Chambersburg PA
CBHW032035040426
42449CB00007B/894